THE
WEAPONS
OF OUR
WARFARE

The Link Family,

May the Lord continue to place His special hedge of protection around you, and keep you strong in the Lord as you press on in your journey of faith.

BY TOM HARMON

Just a field hand
Your servant + friend
Tom
II Tim 2:3+4

THE WEAPONS OF OUR WARFARE
ISBN: 978-1-60920-046-6
Printed in the United States of America
©2012 Tom Harmon
All rights reserved

Cover photo by David De Jong
Edited by Bob English
Proofed by Mary Evenson
Interior design by Ajoyin Publishing, Inc.

"And the seventy returned again with joy, saying, Lord, even the demons are subject to us through thy name. And he said unto them, I beheld Satan as lightning fall from heaven" (Luke 10:17-18).

Library of Congress Cataloging-in-Publication Data

API
Ajoyin Publishing, Inc.
P.O. 342
Three Rivers, MI 49093
www.ajoyin.com

Please direct your inquiries to admin@ajoyin.com

CONTENTS

FOREWORD

There is a battle going on over the souls of men. It is a real battle, a spiritual battle, a battle against a treacherous adversary. Though Satan himself is unseen, his sinister diabolical character is felt throughout the entire world. Satan traffics in evil and markets anything that is opposed to the righteousness of God. Satan is the malignant foe of God and hates everything God stands for. Since God has shown special favor to man by creating him in His own likeness and giving him an eternal spirit, is it any wonder that man is also a special target of Satan's hatred?

God has not left us helpless or alone. He has given us everything we need to walk in victory. The Bible says we can triumph over the worst the ruler of darkness can throw at us. The purpose of this book is to share some basic Scriptural truths that can be used as weapons against the unseen enemy of our souls. Spiritual warfare isn't child's play; it's serious and it's for keeps. We are no match for Satan, but he is no match for Christ.

PREFACE

In 1989 we embarked on an itinerant preaching ministry that has continued to the present. We had no idea of the places we would go or what the Lord would teach us. One of the first things the Lord taught us, however, was spiritual warfare. I must confess that initially I had little to no room for this in my theology. I thought a real devil and demons only existed in Third World countries with the witch doctors. They made for good missionary stories but things like that just didn't happen in the good ol' U.S.A.

As I began to read and study the Scriptures, as well as other books on the subject, the Lord began to give me understanding to some of the struggles in my own life and family. Little did I know that the truth concerning spiritual warfare would increase my faith as well as my understanding of my position in Christ. Both Joyce and I, without hesitation, would say that the truths of spiritual warfare have made the difference between victory and defeat in our marriage and family. In times past when chaos would break out in our relationships, we resisted each other rather than the enemy of our souls to the delight of the devil who would slink away leaving us in a pile of ashes. Once we gained a Biblical understanding of the chaos, we stopped wrestling with each other and entered the battle resisting the real enemy. This resistance always causes him to flee. We are no match for Satan, but he is no match for Christ.

There are many books on the subject of spiritual warfare but all of them, including the book you are about to read, stand in the shadows of "The Christian in Complete Armor" by

William Grunall. It was published in the mid-sixteenth century and continues to stay in print today. A pastor friend recommended it to me about ten years ago and I am so thankful he did. It is not light reading but it is more than worth the effort to strap it on. I highly recommend it to all who are serious in their walk with the Lord and the victory He has provided.

CHAPTER ONE

KNOW YOUR ENEMY

A n enemy is one who is opposed to you—a foe or adversary, one who wishes you injury or destruction, one who longs to see your defeat. The Bible says, "Be sober, be vigilant; because your adversary the devil, as a roaring lion, walketh about, seeking whom he may devour: whom resist steadfast in the faith, knowing that the same afflictions are accomplished in your brethren that are in the world" (1 Pet. 5:8–9).

These two verses contain a lot of insights to the reality of the spiritual battle taking place between the Christian and the devil. First, we are instructed to be sober or serious about the reality of this conflict. To be vigilant means to always bring your "A" game with you. Nothing less will do. Whether the lion is about to roar and spook you towards the waiting pride of lions or stalk and lunge himself from some hidden crouched advantage, one must always be alert to the danger of a potential attack.

The word *adversary* means the one set against you. Just as the Christian has a personal Friend and Helper in the Holy Spirit, he also has a personal enemy and opponent in the devil. There are no neutrals in this conflict, no spectators, only participants. We are either for God and against Satan, or we are for Satan and against God. As we see from verse 9 it is a world class engagement, not something restricted to some remote corner of the planet.

"Whom resist steadfast in the faith" will be the focus of much of this book. "Whom," not what, as though Satan were the name of some abstract force used in a generic way to represent evil.

He is a spirit that has intelligence as well as a diabolical personality and plan. A personality and plan fueled by a genuine hatred for God and His creation. Satan and his plans are to be resisted by the child of God with a faith that is steadfast in the glorious message of the gospel of Christ.

A Spiritual Battle

"Thou therefore endure hardness, as a good soldier of Jesus Christ. No man that warreth entangleth himself with the affairs of this life; that he may please him who hath chosen him to be a soldier" (2 Tim. 2:3–4). There are three things I would like us to consider from this text:

The soldier
The war
The command.

The soldier is one who is engaged in military service having been trained to fight. A soldier is one who has been taught not only the use of arms but also to obey orders, even at the risk of his own life. The soldier is to be daring, courageous and valiant. Valiance is that quality which enables a man to encounter danger with confidence and strength of character. Paul is encouraging

Timothy to be a good soldier by giving him instructions on how best to accomplish it. He warned him not to get all tangled up in the affairs of "this life" if he wants to please Him who has chosen him to be a soldier. Paul is reminding him if he lives to be a hundred, this life is brief at best. Paul's faithful exhortation to Timothy was for him to lay hold of eternal life and fight the good fight of faith, for this is the call of those who profess to know Christ. "Fight the good fight of faith, lay hold on eternal life, unto which thou art also called, and hast professed a good profession before many witnesses" (1 Tim. 6:12).

The war a Christian is chosen by God to fight is a spiritual war and there are many similarities to the wars fought between men on the world stage, such as weapons and strategies. The analytical definition of war is: a hostile encounter, a state of opposition, to contend or strive violently with an adversary, to carry on hostilities with the force of arms, to invade or attack for the purpose of obtaining or establishing superiority or dominion over a foe. The Lord has delivered our spirits from the dominion of darkness and placed us, spiritually, within the kingdom of His dear Son. Yes, we have all spiritual blessings in heavenly places in Christ Jesus. Yet as long as we are on this earth we must contend with the enemy of our souls. We need to be strong in the Lord and the power of His might in order to stand against the schemes of the devil.

The command is to invade the kingdom of darkness with the gospel of light. It is best summed up in the words of Christ, "And Jesus came and spoke unto them saying, All authority is given unto me in heaven and in earth. Go ye, therefore, and teach all nations, baptizing them in the name of the Father, and of the

Son, and of the Holy Spirit, teaching them to observe things whatsoever I have commanded you; and, lo, I am with you always, even unto the end of the age, Amen" (Matt. 28:18–20).

I fear many Christian soldiers are unaware of the seriousness of this battle. Even fewer are trained in how to fight it. The bloodiest battles man has ever fought are by comparison child's play to this war. In the spiritual battle, when a soldier drops his guard, the enemy comes in like a flood. His intent is always the same: steal, kill, and destroy. He delights in encounters that leave the battlefield strewn with the wounded and dying while he carries off the spoils, stolen from his defeated opponents. Not spoils like silver and gold. No, the value of Christian character and principles are more precious to God than all the silver and gold in this world. The unseen enemy of our souls takes advantage of every opportunity. With a vengeance he wreaks bedlam on us until we resist him. By resisting him we put him to flight along with all his wicked works.

THE ORIGIN OF SATAN

Satan is a created being and thus under the authority of his Creator. "In the beginning was the Word, and the Word was with God, and the Word was God. The same was in the beginning with God. All things were made by him; and without him was not anything made that was made" (John 1:1–3). "For by him were all things created, that are in heaven, and that are in earth, visible and invisible, whether they be thrones, or dominions, or principalities, or powers: all things were created by him, and for him: and he is before all things, and by him all things consist" (Col. 1:16–17). The fact that the devil is a created being is most important to understand, for in no way can the created ever usurp authority over the Creator. "And Jesus came and spoke unto them, saying, all authority is given unto me in heaven and in earth. Go ye therefore, and teach all nations, baptizing them in the name of the Father, and of the Son, and of the Holy Spirit: teaching them to observe all things whatsoever I have commanded you: and, lo, I am with you always, even unto the end of the age. Amen (Mt. 28:18–20).

THE FALL OF SATAN

"How art thou fallen from heaven, O Lucifer, son of the morning! How art thou cut down to the ground, who didst weaken the nations! For thou hast said in thine heart, I will ascend into heaven, I will exalt my throne above the stars of God; I will sit also upon the mount of the congregation, in the sides of the north, I will ascend above the heights of the clouds, I will be like the Most High. Yet thou shalt be brought down to hell, to the sides of the pit" (Isa. 14:12–15). These verses obviously refer to Satan who at one time served in the presence of God. His prideful rebellion led him to try and replace God with himself. God cast him out of His presence as Jesus bears testimony to His disciples. He bears testimony having witnessed the scene Himself. "And he said unto them, I beheld Satan as lightening fall from heaven" (Lu. 10:18). It is this verse which gave inspiration for the cover photo.

THE FALL OF ANGELS

We know from Scripture that a certain number of angels were cast out with Satan. In the Olivet discourse when Jesus is describing the end of the age and how the holy angels will be separating the sheep from the goats (saved from the lost), He says, "Then shall the King say unto them on the right hand, Come, ye blessed of my Father, inherit the kingdom prepared for you from before the foundation of the world" (Mt. 25:34). "Then shall he say also unto them on the left hand, Depart from me, ye cursed, into everlasting fire, prepared for the devil and his angels" (Mt. 25:41). Some of the evil angels were sent down to hell and held in chains until the final Day of Judgment. "For if God spared not the angels that sinned, but cast them down to hell, and delivered them into chains of darkness, to be reserved unto judgment" (2 Pet. 2:4). Some of the evil angels, also referred to as demons, were allowed to work under Satan's command in his present war against the kingdom of God. A glimpse into this spiritual battle is seen in the book of Revelation. "And there was war in heaven: Michael and his angels fought against the dragon; and the dragon fought and his angels, and prevailed not; neither was their place found any more in heaven. And the great dragon was cast out, that old serpent, called the Devil, and Satan, who deceiveth the whole world: he was cast out into the earth, and his angels were cast out with him" (Rev. 12:7–9). These evil angels are referred to in Scripture as unclean spirits, familiar spirits, wicked spirits, or demons. If they are given the opportunity they will afflict the children of God. This is spiritual warfare.

THE END OF SATAN

My favorite line from Martin Luther's great old hymn "A Mighty Fortress is Our God" is: *".... for Lo his doom is sure."* In my morning prayers, it has become my custom to always quote a Scripture regarding Satan's doom. I believe it is these Scriptures he fears. "And the devil that deceived them was cast into the lake of fire and brimstone, where the beast and the false prophet are, and shall be tormented day and night forever and ever" (Rev. 20:10). I believe the Scriptures also give insight to the reality that demons fear God. "Thou believest that there is one God; thou doest well: the demons also believe and tremble" (Jas. 2:19). We as children of God need not fear an enemy who has already been defeated; but neither should we become lackadaisical knowing the sinister and diabolical nature of the one who is bent upon being our foe.

Know His Character

To be forewarned is to be forearmed. When one knows his enemy, his personality and character, he is more likely to discern his opponent's actions. This is a substantial advantage both before the fighting begins and in the heat of the battle. I have found the best way to learn about the personality of Satan is to study God. When you know the personality and character of God you can do a 180° opposite and discern the personality and character of Satan. Study the authentic God of the Bible and you will be more apt to spot the counterfeit, even if he tries to disguise himself as an angel of light.

Study God

If God is truth:

"He is the Rock, his work is perfect: for all his ways are justice: a God of truth and without iniquity, just and right is he" (Deut. 32:4).

Then Satan is a liar:

"Ye are of your father the devil, and the lust of your father ye will do. He was a murderer from the beginning, and abode not in the truth, because there is no truth in him. When he speaketh a lie, he speaketh of his own; for he is a liar and the father of it" (John 8:44).

If God is freedom:

"If the Son, therefore, shall make you free, ye shall be free in deed" (John 8:36).

Then Satan is bondage:

"For ye have not received the spirit of bondage again to fear; but ye have received the Spirit of adoption, whereby we cry, Abba, Father" (Rom. 8:15). Satan delights in a world that is obsessed with bondage and addictions of every sort imaginable.

If God is light:

"Then spoke Jesus again unto them, saying, I am the light of the world: he that followeth me shall not walk in darkness, but shall have the light of life" (John 8:12).

If God is life:

"In him was life; and the life was the light of men" (John 1:4).

Then Satan loves darkness:

Darkness is often used as a metaphor for Satan's calling cards, sin and evil. When Judas betrayed Jesus, at possibly earth's darkest hour, Jesus said, "When I was daily with you in the temple, ye stretched forth no hands against me: but this is your hour, and the power of darkness" (Lu. 22:53).

Then Satan is a murderer:

See John 8:44 above. God knows the character of Satan so He makes his boundaries very clear. God told Satan not to kill Job. He was allowed to cover him with boils but not to take his life. "And the Lord said unto Satan, Behold, he is in thine hand; but save his life" (Job 2:6). God made it clear, don't you dare kill him.

If God is love:
"Beloved, let us love one another: for love is of God; and every one that loveth is born of God, and knoweth God. He that loveth not knoweth not God; for God is love" (1 John 4:7–8).

Then Satan's nature is to hate:
The first chapter of Job alone shows his hatred of man, especially a godly man. The first thing he does is kill all of his ten children and almost all of his employees. See Job 1:13–19.

If God is merciful:
"Blessed be the God and Father of our Lord Jesus Christ, who according to his abundant mercy hath begotten us again unto a living hope by the resurrection of Jesus Christ from the dead" (1 Pet. 1:3).

Then Satan is cruel:
Satan is the author of these persecutions, "And others had trial of cruel mocking's and scourging's, yea, moreover of bonds and imprisonment: They were stoned, they were sawn asunder, were tested, were slain with the sword; they wandered about in sheepskins and goatskins; being destitute, afflicted, tormented; (Of whom the world was not worthy:) they wandered in deserts, and in mountains, and in dens and caves of the earth" (Heb. 11:36–38).

If God is holy:

"In the year that King Uzziah died I saw also the Lord sitting upon a throne, high and lifted up, and his train filled the temple. Above it stood the seraphim's: each one had six wings; with two he covered his face, and with two he covered his feet, and with two he did fly. And one cried unto another, and said, Holy, holy, holy, is the Lord of host: the whole earth is full of his glory" (Isa. 6:1–3).

Then Satan is wicked:

"When any one heareth the word of the kingdom, and understandeth it not, then cometh the wicked one, and catcheth away that which was sown in his heart. This is he which received seed by the way side" (Mt. 13:19).

If you are interested in a more comprehensive study of the attributes and character of God, I highly recommend "Knowledge of the Holy" by A. W. Tozer. Remember, everything God is in character and personality—Satan is not. If God is Omniscient, then Satan cannot be. If God is Omnipresent, then Satan cannot be. If God is Omnipotent, then Satan cannot be. These may be simple observations but they are absolutely indispensible truths when engaged in a battle with the unseen enemy of our souls.

KNOW HIS GOALS

The Scripture with the most concise description of our enemy's goals is found in the gospel of John. "The thief cometh not, but for to steal, and to kill, and to destroy: I am come that they might have life, and that they might have it more abundantly"

(John 10:10). The thief is another name that describes Satan and his character. A thief always takes what doesn't belong to him. On the other hand, God is characterized by giving. "For God so loved the world, that he gave his only begotten Son, that whosoever believeth in him should not perish, but have everlasting life" (John 3:16).

Satan wants to steal every blessing God wants to give us. One such blessing is the blessing of fellowship with Him and the fruit of His Spirit, "But the fruit of his Spirit is love, joy, peace, long-suffering, gentleness, goodness, faith, meekness, temperance: against such there is no law" (Gal. 5:22–23).

Satan also wants to destroy every human relationship that God designed to be meaningful: husband/wife, parent/child, brother/sister. Every relationship whether it is in the work place, neighborhood, or church is his target. He longs to destroy any relationship God has given us.

Satan would kill us physically if he could, but he is equally content for us to commit one of the many forms of suicide so endemic in the world today. He doesn't care if it's mental, emotional, physical, spiritual, relational, social, or financial suicide. Satan is pleased just as long as we destroy ourselves. It is truly sad to see people who are dead while they are living.

Satan's goals are simple and they haven't changed since he showed his hand in the Garden of Eden. Oh, how the goals of the Almighty God are so different from Satan's. I can't help but just now to give thanks to the Lord for the heart He has for people. "I know the thoughts that I think toward you, saith the Lord, thoughts of peace, and not of evil, to give you an expected end" (Jer. 29:11). An expected end—literally a hope and a future.

Know Something of His Devices

Though Satan is cunning and crafty, he is not wise. Wisdom is an attribute of God alone. "Now unto the King eternal, immortal, invisible, the only wise God, be honor and glory forever and ever. Amen" (1 Tim. 1:17). In a battle with the enemy it is a great source of strength to know that we have access to the wisdom of God. The Bible is the Christian soldier's instruction manual in which is kept the wisdom of God.

"For the Lord giveth wisdom:
Out of his mouth cometh knowledge and understanding.
He layeth up sound wisdom for the righteous:
He is a shield to those who walk uprightly.
He keepeth the paths of justice,
And preserveth the way of his saints.
Then thou shalt understand righteousness,
And justice, and equity; yea every good path.
When wisdom entereth into thine heart,
And knowledge is pleasant unto thy soul;
Discretion shall preserve thee,
Understanding shall keep thee:
To deliver thee from the way of the evil man,
From the man that speaketh perverse things"
(Prov. 2: 6–12)

I believe there is wisdom in understanding that Satan uses different devices at different stages in our life. The following is just a glimpse of how the devil plots for our destruction throughout life. Let us consider seven different ages in a person's life.

Devices: From Birth to Ten

Between birth and age ten, a person goes through many changes. He starts out incapable of feeding, clothing, or protecting himself. He needs much care and protection. A word of wisdom: Exercise caution in who watches your children in their early years. Too often Satan gains a subtle foothold through a tare that appears to be wheat. A tare is a plant that looks similar to wheat but it produces absolutely no fruit while all the time stealing precious moisture and nutrients and competing for sunlight. It often dwarfs and sometimes prevents the wheat from producing a healthy crop of grain. "The kingdom of heaven is likened unto a man who sowed good seed in his field: but while men slept, his enemy came and sowed tares among the wheat, and went his way. But when the blade was sprung up, and brought forth fruit, then appeared the tares also. So the servants of the household came and said unto him, Sir, didst not thou sow good seed in thy field? From where then hath it tares? He said unto them, An enemy hath done this. The servant said unto him, Wilt thou then that we go and gather them up? But he said, Nay; lest while ye gather up the tares, ye root up also the wheat with them" (Mt. 13:24–29).

The disciples of Jesus asked Him to explain the parable of the tares of the field and this is what He said, "He that soweth the good seed is the Son of man; the field is the world; the good seed are the children of the kingdom, but the tares are the children of the wicked one; the enemy that sowed them is the devil …" (Mt. 13:37–39). The context of this parable is the end of the age. Regardless of the context, my wife and I saw a bit of wisdom in knowing there are tares among the wheat. The devil would love to catch us sleeping so he might take advantage and sow some of his seed into our children. We came to the conclusion that the best people to care for our children were ourselves. When circumstances demanded otherwise, we exercised the greatest of care. We also realized that between the ages of 7–10, they developed a natural and normal curiosity about themselves. Wisdom seemed to say to us that when it was time for bed, our children would do best in their own home in their own bed, not spending the night with others. We aren't saying we were perfect parents but we never compromised on this one. The older we grow the more we are thankful we didn't. Ultimately, as a parent, you are the one responsible to stand in the gap for your young child against Satan. Teach them what you think is wise regarding the enemy but know that children rarely go off to war on their own. He that hath an ear to hear, let him hear; he that hath an eye to see, let him see.

Devices: From Eleven to Twenty

In the teen years Satan loves to take advantage of the fact that they are young and naïve. When I say naïve, I mean they haven't lived long enough to consider seriously the consequences of their choices. No teenager would ever smoke if he could see himself in his 40's or 50's hacking and coughing with sore lungs and a multitude of health related issues. No teenager would ever smoke his first joint if he could see it opening the door to various drug addictions and destructive lifestyles. This is a time when Satan loves to establish footholds in young people's lives. It's a time when many young people don't have much responsibility. Yet they have plenty of opportunity to live only for the moment. Joyce and I saw wisdom in being transparent with our own past while cautioning them to view the future consequences of present actions. It was a blessed time for us as parents because our faith was strengthened as their faith became real. We shared candidly with them about the enemy and his devices. They learned to fight the devil rather than each other. The devil intended this time of their life for evil but God meant it for good.

DEVICES: FROM TWENTY-ONE TO THIRTY

This time period is characterized by seeking and questioning about the things of life. The rich young ruler in the Bible was more than likely in this age range. He wanted to know what he had to do to inherit eternal life. He didn't want to hear the answer Jesus gave him so he continued his search elsewhere.

This age is a natural time for developing a healthy measure of independence. More often than not, however, the devil takes advantage of this stage by suggesting that they are their own authority; they don't need to be under anyone's authority, least of all God's. If not addressed, footholds surrendered in the teen years can be well on their way to becoming strongholds. Wisdom teaches that if one is to ever have authority in their life they must be under authority.

Jesus marveled at a Roman centurion's understanding of this principle. This man had heard about Jesus' power to heal. Since he had a sick servant, he asked some Jewish friends to entreat Jesus to come and heal his servant. While Jesus was on His way the man came out to meet Him and humbled himself by saying that he was not worthy for Jesus to come under his roof (or under his authority). Let's pick up the narrative there: "Wherefore neither thought I myself worthy to come unto thee: but say in a word, and my servant shall be healed. For I also am a man set under authority, having under me soldiers, and I say to the one, Go, and he goeth; and to another, Come, and he cometh; and to my servant, Do this, and he doeth it. When Jesus heard these things, he marveled at him, and turned him about, and said unto the people that followed him, I say unto you, I have not found so great faith, no, not in all Israel" (Lu. 7:7–9).

DEVICES: FROM THIRTY-ONE TO FORTY

Some of the questions that were being asked in the twenties are answered in the thirties. Major choices are being made about the remainder of life. Usually professions are established and settled into during this age. Family and home values are pretty well established. If a major change is going to be made, more than likely it occurs in this decade. Wisdom seems to say to us that we need to turn a special ear toward heaven and earnestly seek His face for direction. I encourage everyone in this stage of life to do so. By this time of life we are either going God's way or our own way. Satan knows the barrenness of a busy life and you will be busier in this decade than any other time of your life. It can be a very vulnerable time if you compromise the eternal things of life.

This stage of life can be a time for pulling down strongholds. If Satan has a tight grip he will not loosen it easily. This is when you need to draw your weapons and learn how to use them. This is when you become skilled as a soldier. The title of the book, "The Weapons of Our Warfare," was chosen as an encouragement to become proficient in the use of our spiritual arsenal. "I have written unto you, young men, because you are strong, and the word of God abideth in you, and you have overcome the wicked one" (1 John 2:14b).

DEVICES: FROM FORTY-ONE TO FIFTY

By this age you could be well on your way to becoming a good soldier of Jesus Christ. This is the time where you fight your own battles and notch your belt with your own victories. This is the time when you become battle hardened and learn to endure the good fight of faith. "Thou therefore endure hardness, as a good soldier of Jesus Christ" (2 Tim. 2:3). By this time you are not living off someone else's experiences. You have war stories of your own. You are becoming strengthened, established, and settled in the faith. "But the God of all grace, who hath called us unto his eternal glory by Christ Jesus, after that you have suffered awhile, make you perfect, establish, strengthen, settle you" (1 Pet. 5:10). The other side of the coin, however, is if you have not learned to use the weapons of our warfare you could become conditioned with a life of faithlessness and be carried about with every wind of false doctrine.

DEVICES: FROM FIFTY-ONE TO SIXTY

For the most part you have settled in by the time you are in your fifties. Your basic core values of life have been established, either with God or without Him. Often times the devil turns up the pressure to perform. Hypocrisy becomes a greater temptation than normal. Frequently the devil drives people into the wilderness of men-pleasing or worldly pleasure. These rarely satisfy and only seem to have a numbing effect and an aura of meaninglessness. Not many major changes will be made in this decade. You are, for the most part, either pressing on toward God or adrift. Not too many people drift toward God. The good soldier remains steadfast and persevering in the fight. For those who think the battle goes away, I'm sorry to report that it does not. The assaults may not be as often but they are more subtle and ferocious. Wisdom says: stay in the trenches. Endurance is a big gun in this decade and I will write more on it later in the book. "Therefore, my beloved brethren, be ye steadfast, unmovable, always abounding in the work of the Lord, forasmuch as ye know that your labor is not in vain in the Lord" (1 Cor. 15:58).

DEVICES: FROM SIXTY-ONE TO SEVENTY

Saved or lost, people in this decade of life will begin to wonder at the value of their life. Satan loves to come in like a flood with all kinds of questions and doubts. He loves to piggy back on any issue: health, finance, death, changes of any magnitude, large or small. Knowing you are well into the second half of your journey of life gives Satan a great advantage. He loves for Christians to become introspective to a fault, anything to take your eyes off the conquering Savior. In this decade the Christian soldier needs to have a strong grip on the glorious gospel. Hopefully this is a grip he has been strengthening throughout his journey. If one has a good grasp of the gospel, what it is and what it is not, he is more apt to be victorious right on through to the end.

The accuser of the brethren loves to cast doubts especially during this decade. This is when you respond instinctively based on your drill training. After you have done all, you simply continue to stand. "Wherefore take unto you the whole armor of God, that ye may be able to withstand in the evil day, and having done all, to stand. Stand therefore, having your loins girded about with truth, and having on the breastplate of righteousness, and your feet shod with the preparation of the gospel of peace; Above all, taking the shield of faith, with which ye shall be able to quench all the fiery darts of the wicked one. And take the helmet of salvation, and the sword of the Spirit, which is the word of God; Praying always with all prayer and supplication in the Spirit, and watching thereunto with all perseverance and supplications for all saints" (Eph. 6:13–18).

Devices: From Seventy On

For the child of God who has fought the good fight of faith, his latter end is better than his first. This is not to say that Satan gives up or never launches an assault, but it is to say that he has taken some pretty good thrashings and is fearful at the thought of more of the same. If every time you said "hi" to someone and they slugged you in the face, pretty soon you would stop saying "hi." If every time Satan took a shot at you, you responded dressed in armor and skilled in the use of your weapons, he would look for easier pickings.

Physically we don't get better with the passing of time, but spiritually we can. We will wrestle with principalities and powers and rulers of darkness right to the end but we don't have to let them gain the advantage. "Lest Satan should get an advantage of us; for we are not ignorant of his devices" (2 Cor. 2:11) Satan has devices of all shapes and sizes, for both genders, in all cultures, in every age. May God give us wisdom as we press on in our journey of faith. It is God's desire for His children to finish well, but the Bible records many people of faith who didn't. It is truly my desire to finish well. I would love to be able to say at the end of my journey what the Apostle Paul said, "I have fought a good fight, I have finished my course, I have kept the faith; henceforth there is laid up for me a crown of righteousness, which the Lord, the righteous judge, shall give me at that day; and not to me only, but unto all them also who love his appearing" (2 Tim. 4:7–8).

CHAPTER TWO

A BALANCED VIEW
OF THE CONFLICT

Satan loves extremes; he would love to have people either in total denial of his existence or obsessed with him being center stage in everything. In my journey of faith I have visited both extremes. Very early in my walk with the Lord I had no room for a real devil and the powers of darkness. If there were a real devil, he lived in Third World countries with the witch doctors, but certainly not in well-educated America. As I began to study the Scriptures and consider my own struggles, I wondered if possibly Satan could afflict Christians. I began to read some conservative authors on the subject and I was amazed at some of the things they were saying. At one point I think the pendulum swung too far and before I knew it there was a proverbial demon behind every bush. Eventually, the pendulum came to rest where I believe truth is found—in the delicate environment of balance.

A Threefold Arena of Conflict

The Christian fights in a threefold arena of conflict: the world, the flesh and the devil. One of the most concise portions of Scripture to explain this is found in Ephesians. "In which in time past ye walked according to the course of this world, according to the prince of the power of the air, the spirit that now worketh in the sons of disobedience; among whom also we all had our manner of life in times past in the lust of our flesh, fulfilling the desires of the flesh and of the mind, and were by nature the children of wrath, even as others" (vv. 2:2–3). Another enlightening portion is found in the book of James: "But if ye have bitter envying and strife in your hearts, glory not, and lie not against the truth. This wisdom decendeth not from above, but is earthly, sensual, and demonical" (vv. 3:14–15). In this portion the word *"earthly"*—represents the world, *"sensual"*—the flesh, and *"demonical"*—the devil. For some the pull of the world represents their greatest struggle. Others find their main conflict with the flesh. Still others fight hardest against the devil. No one finds a nice evenly proportioned 33.3% warfare on each front. To find victory in each arena requires a different strategy with different weapons.

The World

"For God so loved the world, that he gave his only begotten Son, that whosoever believeth in him should not perish, but have everlasting life" (John 3:16). The word *world* here refers to the created earth and especially mankind created with an eternal spirit in God's likeness. In other portions of Scripture however, the word world has another meaning. After the temptation of man and his fall into sin, Satan became the prince or ruler of this world. He usurped the authority God had given to man. Earth became a place where Satan took every God-created institution and twisted it with his evil nature. The word *world* also refers to the earth which is now under the domain and control of Satan.

Art is a God-created institution for His glory; Satan has obviously touched it and in all too many cases made it worldly. He has twisted it into something that is used to turn people away from God.

Literature is a God-created institution used to glorify God on so many occasions. Yet Satan has touched it and contaminated it with such vile communications. I wish I hadn't read some of the junk I have read. Reading is a powerful medium for getting stuff into the mind. Once it's in the mind though it's not always easy to get it out.

Science is a God-created institution. Yet Satan has taken it and used it to replace the God Who designed the laws of science.

Government is a God-created institution. When we look at the governments of the world though, we see the devil's fingerprints all over them. God knew that man would need government so He instituted if for our good. But now whether the government is one run "by the people and for the people" or one that is run as a monarchy, Satan's touch has corrupted them all.

Medicine is a God-designed institution. But the touch of the god of this world has turned it into an enterprise.

We could go on and on: education, technology, business, sports, philanthropy, retirement, etc. "Beware lest any man spoil you through philosophy and vain deceit, after the tradition of men, after the rudiments of the world, and not after Christ" (Col. 2:8).

Religion—Satan has even gone so far as to spread a perverted gospel. "I marvel that you are so soon removed from him that called you into the grace of Christ unto another gospel, which is not another; but there are some that trouble you, and would pervert the gospel of Christ" (Gal. 1:6–7). "But if our gospel be hidden, it is hidden to them that are lost, in whom the god of this world hath blinded the minds of them who believe not, lest the light of the glorious gospel of Christ, who is the image of God, should shine unto them" (2 Cor. 4:3–4).

A Christian has dual citizenship, one in heaven and the other on earth. "For our citizenship is in heaven, from which also we look for the Savior, the Lord Jesus Christ" (Phil. 3:20). But the fact remains we are also citizens of earth. We are citizens in the midst of a crooked and perverse nation among whom we are to shine as lights in the world.

The world can have a strong pull on the Christian soldier and the apostles knew it. The Apostle John writes, "Love not the world, neither the things that are in the world. If any man love the world, the love of the Father is not in him. For all that is in the world, the lust of the flesh, and the lust of the eyes, and the pride of life, is not of the Father, but is of the world. And the world passeth away, and the lust of it; but he that doeth the will of God abideth forever" (1 John 2:15–17).

Demas was once one of the Apostle Paul's faithful co-laborers in the gospel, yet he reports in his last letter to Timothy, "For Demas hath forsaken me, having loved this present world, and is departed unto Thessalonica …" (2 Tim. 4:10). Demas was from the bustling city of Thessalonica and his name means "popular." I must confess that as an American Christian I too am more worldly than I should be. All too often the good seed of God's Word falls among thorns in my life. The thorns which are the cares of this world and the deceitfulness of riches choke out the Word and it becomes unfruitful.

DEALING WITH WORLDLINESS

"Pure religion and undefiled before God and the Father is this: to visit the fatherless and the widows in their affliction, and to keep oneself unspotted from the world" (Jas.1:27). How does a Christian keep the world from rubbing off on him? How can a Christian be in the world and yet not _of_ the world? How do you fight its relentless influence? I have a long way to go but I have found great help in these two simple truths. I recommend them, knowing that more mature Christians have found these truths offer even greater depth than I have experienced.

First: "I beseech you therefore brethren, by the mercies of God, that you present your bodies a living sacrifice, holy, acceptable unto God, which is your reasonable service. And be not conformed to this world; but be ye transformed by the renewing of your mind, that ye may prove what is that good and acceptable, and perfect, will of God" (Rom. 12:1–2). We have no sure understanding of the will of God apart from the word of God. The third book I wrote, "By the Word of God," gives a plan for making the Word a part of your life. The chapter titles are:

"Read it Daily"
"Study it Carefully"
"Memorize it Intentionally"
"Meditate on it Continually"
"Share it Lovingly" and
"Obey it Passionately"

The Word of God has a transforming and cleansing effect on our mind. Just as we are in the world daily, we need to be in the Word of God daily.

Second: "For whatever is born of God overcometh the world; and this is the victory that overcometh the world, even our faith" (1 John 5:4). Being in the Word of God is not the end. It is the beginning. It is through the Word that the Holy Spirit teaches us how to be godly in this present world. The Spirit of God takes the Word of God and shows us the ways of God. "Show me thy ways, O Lord; teach me thy paths" (Psa. 25:4). "Thy word is a lamp unto my feet, and a light unto my path" (Psa. 119:105). God will show you His path and He will even walk it with you. But He will not walk it for you. He reveals truth and after that comes faith. "So then faith cometh by hearing, and hearing by the word of God" (Rom. 10:17). If a man says he has faith but there is no evidence of his faith he is only kidding himself. We live what we believe. All the rest is just religious talk. When the Word of God speaks contrary to my lifestyle then I must change. I cry out to God for help and then say, "let the slugfest of faith begin." Faith continues to remain the substance of things hoped for and the evidence of things not seen.

The Flesh

The word "flesh" used in Ephesians chapter 2 verse 3 as well as in many other portions of the New Testament is making reference to the human nature that is deprived of the Spirit of God, dominated by sin. It is the only nature we are born with. "Behold, I was shaped in iniquity, and in sin did my mother conceive me" (Psa. 51:5). This is why we don't have to teach our children how to be selfish, pout, get angry, lie, take toys from others just to be mean, or a host of other behaviors that we, as parents, like to think we never had. The simple truth is their nature came straight from us. Ours came from our parents and on back as far as Adam.

Adam was made without a sin nature. He was created holy and in perfect fellowship with God. How could Adam have sinned without a sin nature or any worldly influence? It took an outside influence to get him to sin. That outside influence was Satan in the form of a serpent. He tempted Adam and Eve to doubt God's Word. Then he flat out called God a liar. He accused God of withholding something better from them than what they already had. "And the serpent said unto the woman, Ye shall not surely die; for God doth know in the day that ye eat thereof, then your eyes shall be opened, and ye shall be as God, knowing good and evil" (Gen. 3:4–5). He enticed them with the thought of being independent from God, being the captain of their own ship and the master of their own destiny. This was the very issue for which God had Satan cast out of heaven. Reluctant as we are to admit it, our human nature comes from none other than the father of lies, the devil. This nature is locked very deep within the center of man's soul and nothing apart from the grace of God can reveal it, causing us to run to Him for mercy and forgiveness.

THE CARDIOLOGIST'S REPORT

God has demonstrated His love for man throughout history. He is not willing that any should perish, but that all should come to repentance. Repentance is turning away from our desire to be independent from God. That desire, to be independent from God, is the host that hatches a multitude of vile thoughts and actions. Jesus knew this to be true of all men even the very people who were witness to His mighty miracles. "Now when Jesus was in Jerusalem at the Passover, in the feast day, many believed in his name, when they saw the miracles which he did. But Jesus did not commit himself unto them, because he knew all men, and needed not that any should testify of man; for he knew what was in man" (John 2:23–25). In Mark chapter 7, the Pharisees jump all over Jesus because they observed His disciples eating without going through the ceremonial washing of hands. The Pharisees said His men were defiled according to the tradition of the elders. Jesus used this opportunity to give a clear diagnosis of the nature of man's heart. "And he saith unto them, Are ye so without understanding also? Do ye not perceive, that whatever thing from outside entereth into the man it cannot defile him; because it entereth not into his heart, but the stomach, and then goeth out into the draught, purging all foods? And he said, That which cometh out of the man, that defileth the man. For from within, out of the heart of men, proceed evil thoughts, adulteries, fornication, murders, thefts, covetousness, wickedness, deceit, lasciviousness, an evil eye, blasphemy, pride, foolishness. All these evil things come from within, and defile the man" (vv. 18–23). I am resistant to this Biblical diagnosis of my heart because of my sin, but all too often I am forced to admit it.

The Whopper

My dear wife had me on a diet and I had agreed to eat only what she set in front of me. She had me on a cabbage soup diet. I like cabbage and I like soup so I didn't anticipate any problems, but after about three days the novelty wore off. As the story goes, I had been in Lansing running some errands. On my way home, as I got off the expressway which has a half dozen typical fast food restaurants and just as I was about to turn north on M-52, I saw the Burger King sign that read, "Whoppers 99¢." I thought to myself that I would have just one and nobody would be the wiser. Now I was hungry and one whopper doesn't come close to taking the edge off the appetite of a guy my size. My rationale was that I had been doing well for three days; one whopper wouldn't do me any harm. I thought I won't tell Joyce if she doesn't ask. I felt I was being deceitful but not "that bad." The new man kicked in with the thought that, if I was going to violate our agreement then I would have to tell her. The old man said, "just let it ride and don't say anything about it." As I went through the drive-thru, I ordered two. After all, it was such a good deal. If I was going to keep quiet about one whopper I might as well keep silent about two. I hurriedly ate them both and made sure there wasn't any mayonnaise on my shirt or chin. I entered the house and said, "I'm hungry, what's for lunch?" Joyce announced it was cabbage soup. I ate it like I was starving and almost made it through the meal when I'm sure the Holy Spirit prompted Joyce to ask if I had eaten anything. I calmly said no. It came out quickly and without a stutter. The only thing I was lacking was a halo. As soon as I told the lie, the Holy Spirit said He had just seen me eat two whoppers. He told me I was going to have to tell Joyce that I had lied to her, what the lie was, and ask her forgiveness. I negotiated with the

Lord for about five minutes using my standard excuses. I told Him I wouldn't do it again, etc. etc. The devil's voice was quick to tell me if I admitted lying to her, she would never believe me again. I knew my fellowship with the Lord was directly related to my fellowship with my wife. I knew the devil loves secrecy while God loves transparency, so I asked God for mercy and cleansing for my sin against Him. I asked Him for grace to make it right with Joyce. I humbled myself before Joyce and told her I had lied about not having anything to eat before lunch. I told her I had a whopper. The Holy Spirit moaned His disapproval in my ear. I quickly told her the truth, I really had eaten two. The old man likes to come clean in stages revealing how he hangs on to his sin. Joyce was obviously disappointed and asked me why I had done this. I told her I had just asked God the same question and His answer was clear: I am a liar at heart. "The heart is deceitful above all things, and desperately wicked; who can know it? I the Lord search the heart, I test the conscience, even to give every man according to his ways, and according to the fruit of his doings" (Jer. 17:9–10).

Within a few moments Joyce said to me. "Tom, it is good to see God at work in your life. He is at work in my life as well." She admitted times of struggling with being deceitful over things and fearful of humbling herself. She said all of us want others to think better of us than we really are, it's just human nature. She also said it's good to know that if you tell me the truth over something small like this, then I know you will tell me the truth in bigger things as well. "He that is faithful in that which is least is faithful also in much; and he that is unjust in the least is unjust also in much" (Lu. 16:10).

One mystery that remains unsolved by man is the mystery of man's capacity for evil. The Biblical doctrine of total depravity is the teaching that man has within him the same capacity for evil as Satan himself. In my opinion, it is the most unbelieved doctrine in the Bible even though it is played out on the world's stage every day of our lives.

Two Natures

All of us are born with a human nature. When we are born again we receive a new or divine nature. "Therefore if any man be in Christ, he is a new creation; old things are passed away; behold all things are become new" (2 Cor. 5:17). "According as his divine power hath given unto us all things that pertain to life and godliness, through the knowledge of him that hath called us to glory and virtue; by which are given unto us exceedingly great and precious promises, that by these ye might be partakers of the divine nature, having escaped the corruption that is in the world through lust" (2 Pet. 1:3–4). A Christian then, has two natures living in him. These two are never in agreement on anything. The Holy Spirit would have me walk in the ways of the Lord while my human nature would have me walk to the contrary. Just because a person trusts Christ as his Savior, receives the Holy Spirit and is born again does not mean the old nature with its behavior instantly goes away.

The Apostle Paul shared very candidly his struggle between the old and the new in Romans chapter 7. "For what I do I understand not; but what I would, that do I not; but what I hate, that I do. If then, I do that which I would not, I consent unto the Law that it is good. Now then, it is no more I that do it, but sin that dwelleth in me. For I know that in me, (that is, in my flesh,) dwelleth no good thing; for to will is present with me, but how to perform that which is good I find not" (vv. 15–18). Paul again states that it is not him that acts but the sin that dwells in him. His new man is longing to obey God and bring his behavior in line with his new identity but it just doesn't seem to find a way to do it. "I find then a law, that when I would do good, evil is present with me. For I delight in the law of God after the inward man; But I see another law in my members, warring against the law of my mind, and bringing me into captivity to the law of sin which is in my members" (Rom. 7:21–23). This portion of Scripture makes it very clear that there is a battle going on between the new nature and the old. As Christians we are going to have to step up to the plate and come to grips with the fact that when we want to do good, evil will be closer than our shadow. It is an inescapable law. Sin lives in our members meaning our hands, feet, eyes, ears, nose, mouth, mind, all our body parts.

Almost in despair at the very thought of the battle within himself, Paul makes a powerful and helpful declaration followed by a searching question and a profound answer. "O wretched man that I am! Who shall deliver me from the body of this death? I thank God through Jesus Christ our Lord. So then with the mind I myself serve the law of God; but with the flesh the law of sin" (Rom. 7:24–25.) We are delivered from the penalty and power of our sin through saving faith in Jesus Christ our Lord but we are not delivered from the presence of our sin. When a person is saved, the next day he wakes up with a new man inside of him. This new man wants to live for God and walk in His righteous ways. He also wakes up in the same sinful body, in the same sinful world, with the same enemy, Satan, to tempt him.

Dealing With the Flesh

You can be in the world but not of the world. You can resist the devil and he will flee from you. But try to get away from yourself. You can't. Everywhere you go, there you are. This is the hardest battleground for me. For some people it's the lure and enticements of the world, for others it's the temptations, oppressions and accusations of the devil, but without hesitation, I can say I am my own worst enemy. Walt Kelly said, "We have met the enemy…and he is us."

One of my favorite and most encouraging portions of Scripture dealing with this subject is found in one of Paul's early epistles, the book of Galatians. "Be not deceived, God is not mocked, for whatever a man soweth, that shall he also reap. For he that soweth to his flesh shall of the flesh reap corruption; but he that soweth to the Spirit shall of the Spirit reap life everlasting. And let us not be weary in well doing; for in due season we shall reap, if we faint not" (Gal. 6:7–9). For most of us our destiny starts with sowing a spiritual thought. You may be asking, "what is a spiritual thought?" Once again I must point you to the Scriptures. The Scripture is given to us by the Spirit of God and contains all kinds of instructions on spiritual thoughts. "Finally, brethren, whatever things are true, whatever things are honest, whatever things are just, whatever things are pure, whatever things are lovely, whatever things are of good report; if there be any virtue, and if there be any praise, think on these things" (Phil. 4:8).

> When you sow a thought, you reap a deed,
> sow a deed, reap a habit,
> sow a habit, reap a character,
> sow a character, reap a destiny.

The principles of sowing and reaping were established by God during the time of creation. These principles include plants always producing after their own kind. In other words, we reap what we sow. Another obvious truth is we reap in a different season than we sow. No one plants a tomato seed in the ground one day and expects to harvest a tomato the next. The seed has to germinate. It sprouts. The plant grows. It blossoms and eventually it yields fruit. It is a God-created truth, a principle in the law of sowing and reaping. It takes time for spiritual seeds to mature and produce their fruit as well. If you read your Bible one day, don't expect to become a theologian the next.. The same truth applies to prayer, marriage, family, ministry, finances, work ethics, and so on. I'm sure that is why God included the admonition to not become weary in well doing, for in due season we will reap. We will reap if only we don't faint.

The tendency is to become discouraged after a few weeks of sowing to the Spirit and then give up. Not very many things produce a crop in three weeks. I guess you can grow mushrooms in around that time if you feed them manure and keep them in the dark. Not a very good analogy of the Christian life. Psalms 1 gives us a much better picture.

"Blessed is the man who walketh not in the counsel of the ungodly, nor standeth in the way of sinners, nor sitteth in the seat of the scornful.

But his delight is in the law of the Lord; and in his law he doth meditate day and night.

And he shall be like a tree planted by the rivers of water, that bringeth forth its fruit in its season; its leaf also shall not wither; and whatsoever he doeth shall prosper" (vv. 1–3).

An fruit farmer once told me that it takes about ten years

for a fruit tree to begin to pay back all the labor and expense that went into it. From seeds to saplings, after adding fertilizers, herbicides, and insecticides, after surviving frosts, pruning's, and the harvest, eventually it begins to show a profit. All throughout Scripture we are admonished to be patient. "Be patient therefore brethren, unto the coming of the Lord. Behold, the farmer waiteth for the precious fruit of the earth, and hath long patience for it, until he receive the early and latter rain. Be ye also patient, establish your hearts; for the coming of the Lord draweth near" (Jas. 5:7–8). Sowing to the Spirit preaches easier than it lives out but the truth still remains: you reap what you sow. A life consciously sowing to the Spirit the things of the Spirit will in time produce a Spiritual harvest, a crop where one has power over the flesh. "This I say then, walk in the Spirit, and ye shall not fulfill the lust of the flesh" (Gal. 5:16).

THE DEVIL

In the first decade of my journey of faith, I had some measurable success in dealing with the world. I even saw some progress in warring with the flesh. But I remained in absolute ignorance with regard to the devil and his assaults against me. I would have seasons of growth and even strength, then suddenly I would be blindsided from an unguarded flank. I felt like I'd been hammered back to square one. When I came to understand that I had to face three fronts and that each one had to be fought differently, I took courage. It was a slow start but steady. Wrestling with an unseen enemy required faith I hadn't yet known. I knew nothing of the armor and precious little of the weapons and how to use them. Some of the things I have learned and continue to learn will be the focus of the remainder of this book.

CHAPTER THREE

THE ARMOR OF GOD

No portion of Scripture details the armor of God as thoroughly as Paul's letter to the church at Ephesus. The church at Ephesus consisted of converts with a background in occult worship. We know from the book of Acts that many artisans made large profits from the pagan worship of the fertility goddess Diana. Satan had a stronghold in Ephesus through magical arts and people who specialized in the demonic practices of the underworld. How much of a stronghold did Satan have? After Paul spent three years working with these new believers helping them grow strong in the Lord and the power of His might, the following is recorded. "And many that believed came, and confessed, and showed their deeds. Many of those also who used magical arts brought their books together, and burned them before all men; and they counted the price of them, and found it fifty thousand pieces of silver" (Acts 19:18–19). A piece of silver probably refers to a Greek drachma which represented a laborer's daily wage. Today at a $15.00 per hour wage a laborer earns a daily wage of $120. At that rate 50,000 drachma would equal approximately $6 million. Knowing these people would spend such an amount on magic and sorcery is no small

41

statement to the influence Satan had in their daily lives. Ephesus was a satanic stronghold, but a stronghold which fell to the power of the gospel.

As Paul concludes his letter to the Ephesians, he reminds them again of that spiritual aspect of the battle. "Finally, my brethren, be strong in the Lord, and in the power of his might. Put on the whole armor of God, that ye may be able to stand against the wiles of the devil" (Eph. 6:10–11). The word "wiles" means the well-rehearsed tricks or deceptions in which the devil is so skilled. Paul makes it clear that God Himself has designed each piece of armor for the Christian soldier. Every piece has a special function and every soldier is required to put on his complete suit. "For we wrestle not against flesh and blood, but against principalities, against powers, against the rulers of the darkness of this world, against spiritual wickedness in high places, wherefore take unto you the whole armor of God, that you may be able to withstand in the evil day, and having done all, to stand. Stand therefore, having your loins girded about with truth, and having on the breastplate of righteousness; and your feet shod with the preparation of the gospel of peace; Above all, taking the shield of faith, with which ye shall be able to quench all the fiery darts of the wicked. And take the helmet of salvation, and the sword of the Spirit, which is the word of God; Praying always with all prayer and supplication in the Spirit, and watching thereunto with all perseverance and supplication for all saints" (Eph. 6:13–18). These are clearly detailed instructions for the Christian soldier involved in a spiritual battle against Satan.

ABOVE ALL

The emphasis of this book is the weapons of our warfare and yet I wish to address one piece of armor before we get to the weapons. That piece is the shield of faith. God himself becomes a shield around those whom He has redeemed. When Abraham, who through the righteousness of faith (see Rom. 4:13) obeyed God's word, he left Ur of the Chaldeans and went to a land that he knew not. He went literally to a land where he was a stranger without any rights as a citizen, (see Heb. 11:8). It was in that place God told him He would be a shield for him. "After these things the word of the Lord came to Abram in a vision, saying, Fear not, Abram; I am thy shield, and thy exceeding great reward" (Gen. 15:1). Hebrews 11 is filled with accounts of the exploits of men and women of faith. David was also a man of faith and knew the Lord to be his shield, "But thou, O Lord, art a shield for me; my glory, and the lifter up of mine head" (Psa. 3:3). Paul in Romans 4 uses these two Old Testament saints, Abraham and David, as examples of the greatest kind of faith.

Justifying Faith

The greatest kind of faith is justifying faith. When a person, young or old, male or female, realizes through the gospel that they can have their sins forgiven and now stand justified before the righteous Judge of all the earth, Oh, what joy and peace. "Much more then, being now justified by His blood, we shall be saved from wrath through Him" (Rom. 5:9). When a person hears the gospel of Christ and responds to the call of God to faith alone in Christ alone, he is sealed by the Holy Spirit until the day of redemption. "In whom ye also trusted, after ye heard the word of truth, the gospel of your salvation; in whom also after ye believed, ye were sealed with that Holy Spirit of promise" (Eph. 1:13). Oh, what peace it is to know that you have been justified freely by grace through faith. "Being justified freely by his grace through the redemption that is in Christ Jesus: Whom God hath set forth to be a propitiation through faith in his blood, to declare his righteousness for the remission of sins that are past, through the forbearance of God; To declare, I say, at this time his righteousness; that he might be just, and the justifier of him who believeth in Jesus. Where is boasting then? It is excluded. By what law? Of works? Nay: but by the law of faith. Therefore we conclude that a man is justified by faith without the deeds of the law" (Rom. 3:24–28).

No wonder Paul was not ashamed of the gospel of Christ. He knew it to be the power of God unto salvation to everyone who believed it. "For in it is the righteousness of God revealed from faith to faith; as it is written, The just shall live by faith" (Rom. 1:17). Hearing the gospel is no sure guarantee of salvation. "For unto us was the gospel preached, as well as unto them; but the word preached did not profit them, not being mixed with faith in them that heard it" (Heb. 4:2). Another way of saying this is, the gospel is not salvation. salvation is what occurs when the gospel is believed, but the gospel is the gospel whether it is believed or not. Both the gospel and faith are necessary in salvation. Another point of clarification about faith is that faith in faith will not save you, only faith in Christ will bring you peace with God. "Therefore being justified by faith, we have peace with God through our Lord Jesus Christ; by whom also we have access by faith into this grace in which we stand, and rejoice in hope of the glory of God" (Rom. 5:1–2).

THE IMPORTANCE OF FAITH

Of all the graces the Christian soldier needs to embrace, faith is at the top of the pile. One may rush to 1 Corinthians 13 and beg to differ. "And now abideth faith, hope, love, these three, but the greatest of these is love" (1 Cor. 13:13). However, most commentators agree that the context in which love is the greatest is in heaven. In heaven there will be no need for either faith or hope, so love will abide forever. When in heaven we will be beyond the devil's reach, there will be no more need of a shield because the last battle will have been fought and the victory won. But while we are upon earth, now abiding, there is still much need of the all-important shield of faith.

Faith protects all the other parts of the armor. The shield of faith is basically armor upon armor. It is no wonder when Jesus was about to go to the cross, leaving Peter to undergo his worst assault by Satan, Jesus prayed for his faith not to fail. He didn't pray that his love wouldn't fail, or that his patience wouldn't fail, or any of the other virtues. Jesus prayed for Peter's <u>faith</u>. "And the Lord said, Simon, Simon, behold Satan hath desired to have you, that he may sift you as wheat; but I have prayed for thee, that thy faith fail not. And when thou art converted, strengthen the brethren" (Lu. 22:31–32). During those next 72 hours, Satan sent his very worst against Peter. He was attacked by a spirit of fear helping him to deny the Lord. When he cursed the Lord on his third denial you can be sure the devil heaped unbearable guilt and condemnation on him. He was in a world of confusion as he wept bitterly, tormented by the accuser of the brethren. I dare say he heard the accusing lies of Satan telling him God was harsh and cruel, unforgiving and merciless, wanting him to doubt every truth he had learned in the past three years. Satan convinced Judas to take his own life and it wouldn't surprise me if he suggested the same thing to Peter. But Jesus prayed that his faith wouldn't fail. He knew that Peter's faith would quench all the fiery darts of the wicked one. It didn't keep the fiery darts from coming but eventually they were extinguished. Within only a few weeks Peter was preaching his first Holy Spirit-filled sermon where 3,000 responded in faith and were saved.

Scripture records that Jesus only marveled at two things: faith and the lack of faith. A centurion understood that to have authority one had to be under authority. Even Nicodemus recognized that no man could do the miracles that Jesus was doing except God was with Him. The centurion had faith in Jesus that He was under the authority of God. Jesus hadn't come to do His own thing but the will of the Father. Jesus marveled and said of the centurion that He hadn't seen so great faith, no, not in all of Israel, (see Lu. 7:9). Jesus was marveled by faith but when in His home town of Nazareth He marveled at something else. He would have performed more miracles among them but for their lack of faith. There He marveled at their unbelief, (see Mk. 6:6).

Established in the Faith

"As ye have therefore received Christ Jesus the Lord, so walk ye in him; rooted and built up in him, and established in the faith, as ye have been taught, abounding therein with thanksgiving" (Col. 2:6–7). We receive Christ by grace through faith and we are supposed to live according to the same principle. Eventually we are to become established in the faith. In the introduction of Paul's second letter to the church at Thessalonica he said that he heard their faith was growing exceedingly (see 2 Thess. 1:3). They were becoming established in the faith. "Watch, stand fast in the faith, quit ye like men, be strong" (1 Cor. 16:13). When a person's behavior begins to line up with what they say they believe, then their faith is becoming established in the faith. The world is sick of our Christian theology; they want to see our faith. "Now faith is the substance of things hoped for, the evidence of things not seen" (Heb. 11:1).

When children obey their parents it is a special blessing to all in the home. When we were with our children they would almost always obey our voice; rarely would they resist our rule in our presence. This was a special blessing and we look back with gratefulness for their submission to our authority. As they grew older we learned of their obedience to the things we had said when we were not present. We were even more grateful when we heard that. "Wherefore, my beloved brethren, as ye have always obeyed, not as in my presence only, but now much more in my absence, work out your own salvation with fear and trembling. For it is God who worketh in you both to will and to do of his good pleasure" (Phil. 2:12–13).

THE SHIELD OF FAITH

I have come to think of the shield of faith as obedience to objective truth. For the Christian soldier, the Bible is that objective truth. Obedience consists of our submission to the Bible. Faith is a doing thing that becomes evidence in the court of our lives. It is evidence for our case that we have true biblical faith. "Even so faith, if it hath not works, is dead being alone. Yea, a man may say, Thou hast faith, and I have works; show me thy faith without thy works, and I will show thee my faith by my works. Thou believest that there is one God; thou doest well: the demons believe also and tremble. But wilt thou know, O vain man, that faith without works is dead?" (Jas. 2:17–20). The only thing deader than faith without works is works without faith. Have you ever considered that it is possible to have Christian works without Christ? No work I have ever done or will ever do has saving efficacy. "For what saith the scripture? Abraham believed God, and it was counted unto him for righteousness. Now to him that worketh is the reward not reckoned of grace, but of debt. But to him that worketh not, but believeth on him that justifieth the ungodly, his faith is counted for righteousness" (Rom. 4:3–5). A true work of faith does not show my independence from God but rather my absolute dependence upon Him. I can do all things through Christ who strengthens me but I also know that without Him I can do nothing, Phil. 4:13.

When as a soldier I am tempted to disobey an obvious command of Christ (whether through satanic temptation, the world's strong pull, the inner rebellions of the flesh, or possibly the working of all three simultaneously, as is often the case), the fiery darts will not be quenched if the shield of faith is not in place. Incendiary darts start fires that get out of control quickly and before you know it, all hell seems to have broken out in your life. The shield of faith is the one piece of armor that needs to be in place at all times. "See then that ye walk circumspectly, not as fools, but as wise, redeeming the time, because the days are evil" (Eph. 5:15–16). Obedience to the Word of God when others are watching is a good thing, but obedience to the same truth when no one is watching is even better. Accountability to man is a helpful thing, but accountability to God when only you and He are present is a powerful shield against the enemy. That kind of faith is a soldier's mark of strength. "I have written unto you young men because you are strong, and the word of God abideth in you and ye have overcome the wicked one" (1 John 2:14b).

STRONG IN FAITH

It takes time to grow strong in faith and skilled with your shield. It takes patience to develop endurance. Abraham wasn't always strong in faith. Scripture records a time when he lied about Sarah being his sister and neglected to mention that she was also his wife. It also speaks of a time when he agreed with Sarah in a conspiracy to use Hagar to help God keep His promise of a child. As he grew older however, his faith became stronger. "And being not weak in faith, he considered not his own body now dead, when he was about a hundred years old, neither yet the deadness of Sarah's womb. He staggered not at the promise of God through unbelief, but was strong in faith, giving glory to God; and being fully persuaded that, what he had promised, he was able also to perform" (Rom. 4:19–21). His faith grew to a point that when God asked him to offer his son, the promised son of faith, Isaac, as a burnt offering, he obeyed. Abraham knew that Isaac was the son through whom God would bless all the nations of the world. He believed God was able to raise Isaac up from the ashes if He wanted to. "By faith Abraham, when he was tested, offered up Isaac; and he that had received the promises offered up his only begotten son, of whom it was said , That in Isaac shall thy seed be called; Accounting that God was able to raise him up, even from the dead, from which also he received him in a figure" (Heb. 11:17–19). Oh, how Satan must have hated to see such faith in Abraham. I'm sure that Satan must have reached deep into his arsenal and let everything he had fly, but Abraham's shield of faith did as the Scriptures promised. It quenched all the fiery darts shot at him. We see that Abraham was no longer weak in faith; he became a seasoned veteran, skilled with the shield of faith. He was an experienced soldier but that doesn't mean Satan never fired another fiery dart his way.

Caution

The battle isn't over 'til it's over. Just because we become skilled with our shield of faith don't think the enemy is going to stop firing at us. Just look at the book of Job chapters 1 and 2. There is no decade of our lives when Satan is going to leave us alone. As we grow older and change, and things do change, so does the style in which he presents his temptations and lies. It is good for us to know that Satan is not omniscient. He does not know everything. He is simply a student of human behavior. He observes us and draws conclusions as to the status of our heart based on our walk with the Lord, good or bad. He learns our strengths and weakness and even gets to know our personality. He will draft his plan of attack based on our strengths and weaknesses. You don't have to be a military genius to understand that makes him a formidable foe. The unseen enemy of our souls would love nothing more than to have our scalps hanging from his belt. He will use every diabolical trick in his evil nature to ensnare and destroy our testimony for Christ. Though he is not to be reverenced, he is not to be ignored either.

The Help of an Eternal Perspective

"Fight the good fight of faith, lay hold on eternal life, unto which thou art also called, and hast professed a good profession before many witness" (1 Tim. 6:12). "And the devil that deceived them was cast into the lake of fire and brimstone, where the beast and the false prophet are, and shall be tormented day and night forever and ever" (Rev. 20:10). Take heart good soldier: the battle lasts but only a breath. In that breath, consider Him who endured the best Satan could throw at Him. He prevailed and because He did we also can experience the victory He has provided.

CHAPTER FOUR

THE MOST POWERFUL WEAPON IN YOUR ARSENAL

A good soldier is one who is aware of his general's commands and is determined to be alert at all times to carry them out. We are commanded to be strong in the Lord and the power of His might. This is not a new command but very much like the one given by Moses to the whole nation of Israel including its leaders. "<u>Be strong</u> and of a good courage, fear not, nor be afraid of them; for the Lord thy God, he it is who doth go with thee; he will not fail thee, nor forsake thee" (Deut. 31:6). In the next verse a special charge is given to Joshua who is about to become the one to replace Moses as national leader. "And Moses called unto Joshua, and said unto him in the sight of all Israel, <u>Be strong</u> and of a good courage; for thou must go with this people unto the land which the Lord hath sworn unto their fathers to give them, and thou shalt cause them to inherit it" (v. 7). Joshua was a man who knew how to fight and win battles. He was also a man who was strong in the Lord and the power of His might. Joshua means *Yahweh (Jehovah) saves*. Is it any wonder that God chose the name Joshua for the name of His son, Jesus? For Jesus is the Greek rendering of the Hebrew name "Yahweh saves"? I would also like to say that I believe the book of Joshua is probably the best warfare manual in the Bible. I will explain more on that later when we discuss our spiritual weapons.

Remember that within our sphere of influence there will always be people who need us to be strong. The greatest strength we can offer them is to be strong in the Lord and the power of His might. We are to put on the whole armor of God so that we may be able to stand against the wiles of the devil. The word "wiles" is the Greek *methodeia*. In this context, it refers to the devil's scheming craftiness, his strategies and methods. The devil is crafty and constantly scheming, but there is one strategy he seems to delight in more than any other—temptation. Temptation is a method by which he tries to entice us to do evil. He is called the tempter in Matthew 4:3 and 1 Thessalonians 3:5. Temptation is at the heart of his devices and they are well rehearsed. All too often they are carried out with polished precision.

The Process of Temptation

In James chapter 1, we see the process all people experience when they are tempted. It is good for the soldier to remember this process so he might be the wiser when he finds himself in it. "Let no man say when he is tempted, I am tempted of God; for God cannot be tempted with evil, neither tempteth he any man; but every man is tempted, when he is drawn away of his own lust, and enticed. Then when lust hath conceived, it bringeth forth sin; and sin, when it is finished, bringeth forth death" (Jas. 1:13–15). Let's examine this process from the perspective of a police officer investigating a crime scene.

When the officer arrives at a crime scene, he discovers a dead body and begins to work backward to find the cause and, hopefully, the culprit. Cutting to the chase, we know the cause is sin. The wages of sin has not changed since the fall of man—it's death. Satan lied to us in the garden and we have been dying ever since. He continues to tell us the same lie today. What process brought about that sin? Our original parents had no one but the tempter to bring the sin. He brought it by calling God a liar saying there would be no consequence to eating the forbidden fruit. He sweetened the temptation by promising them they would have their eyes opened to a new truth: they would be like God. They would be independent from God and make their own choices on how they should live, where they could go and what they could do. This strategy is what is referred to in James 1:14 as enticement. For us today it is the sights and sounds of the world that make sin look so appealing and so harmless. It's the fragrances that lure us into the traps of sin. The devil will say, "There is no harm in smelling, or looking or touching, just as long as you don't eat." What really sunk Adam and Eve's ship in this temptation was that the tree was a tree to be desired to make one wise. They already were wise, but this was a tree to make one wiser, even wiser than God. Satan used the very lure that had led to his own downfall. He used that powerful temptation to bring about the downfall of man.

In the garden Satan came to Adam and Eve to get their attention. Through our sinful nature he already has our attention. Every man is drawn away of his own lust. As I said earlier, human nature is the seed of Satan's nature in every one of us. When we enter the process of temptation we do so naturally. I must recognize that when I enter the process of temptation, it is my own desires that turn me toward it. My natural inclination starts the process, though I haven't sinned yet. The world's enticements chime in, and I haven't sinned yet. The devil adds his suggestive pressures, and still I haven't sinned yet. Though now I am very close to it. I sin when my lust conceives; whenever conception occurs be assured the end result will be death. Conception demands union. When my natural lusts have agreement or union with the devil's temptation, the child that comes out of that womb will always be sin resulting in death.

It is important to note that to be tempted is not sin. Jesus was tempted in all points like we are and yet without sin, (see Heb. 4:15). He was in the world sure enough, but He had no sinful inclination or fallen nature. Satan had no part in Him. "Hereafter I will not talk much with you; for the prince of this world cometh, and hath nothing in me" (John 14:30). We are not in sin by virtue of just being in the world or being prone to wander. Sinful actions result when we agree with the Tempter. There are times when this process occurs rather quickly and then there are times when it can take months or even years. "Blessed is the man that endureth temptation; for when he is tried, he shall receive the crown of life, which the Lord hath promised to them that love him" (Jas. 1:12).

The process of temptation is not sin itself, but unless we break the process it always leads to sin. There is a way though to stay out of the process. Remember, the process begins when we are drawn away. Since we can only go one direction at a time, if we are drawing near to God, we cannot be drawn away. "Submit yourselves therefore to God, resist the devil, and he will flee from you. Draw near to God, and he will draw near to you" (Jas. 4:7–8a). The first and most important part of drawing near to God is submitting yourself to Him. In a prayer of faith you tell Him you place yourself under the authority of His Word and ask Him for grace to help you walk in the Spirit. God is not playing some cosmic game of hide and seek but wants to have fellowship with you. God is not so concerned with where you are in your journey of faith as He is with *what direction* you are facing. If you have turned toward Him then start walking in what truth He gives you and He will do more than meet you half way. As you begin to grow in the grace and knowledge of the Lord Jesus, you will know what it means to draw near to Him and have Him draw near to you.

ACCUSATION:
ONE OF SATAN'S FAVORITE MANEUVURES

Satan tempts us in many ways, thus the plural, "wiles." One of his favorite ways is to accuse God to us and us to God. Satan accused Job to God that he would curse Him to His face if God lowered His hedge of protection. Satan will accuse God to us as he did with Peter as he launched his merciless assault on his faith. Satan sends his fiery darts into the piles of satanic waste that are just part and parcel of being a citizen of earth. These heaps of rubbish—doubt, temptations, accusations, and lies—are all about us and most of them are extremely flammable. The following account is an example of the process of this temptation.

THE BIG WEAPON

Recently, I came under one of Satan's attacks which I hadn't experienced in many years. Bless God it backfired on the enemy. Hopefully those who read this account will be strengthened in the Lord and the power of His might. Hopefully you may be a little better prepared to take your own stand in a similar conflict.

This past autumn while I was reading the section on hypocrisy in Volume Two of William Grunall's, "The Christian in Complete Armor," I began to become introspective to a fault. Remember, the devil loves extremes and hates reason or balance. I over-examined my works and under-examined the works of Christ. I was alone in my study and before I knew it I was kneeling with my head in my chair and praying, "Oh God, if I am not a true Christian, Lord, I want to be." No sooner than the prayer had come out of my mouth, in that very instant, the Holy Spirit rose up big in me and I proclaimed my hope in Christ and Him alone—If I am not justified by grace through faith in Christ and what He has done for me then I will never be justified by what I can do for Him. Tears of joy filled my eyes and my spirit began to soar like an eagle. I rejoiced with many hallelujahs to God my Savior.

After ten minutes or so of worshiping God in Spirit and in Truth, another wave of His goodness began to flow over me. I said to myself that I had not questioned my salvation in over thirty years. I instantly saw the tempter's fingerprints all over this. I recalled the first temptation of Christ in the wilderness. "And when the tempter came to him, he said, If thou be the Son of God, command that these stones be made bread" (Mt. 4:3). I remember thinking the enemy must be insane to try and get the incarnate Son of God to question Who He was, or to tempt Him to do something supernatural to prove His identity. Instead of falling for the temptation Jesus took the offensive and drew the Sword of the Spirit and put the enemy on the retreat. Satan doesn't have much accuracy with his darts of doubt while he himself is dodging the blows of a two-edged sword in the hand of a skilled warrior. Scripture memory paid off and in a flash I had Titus 3:5, Ephesians 2:8–9, Romans 4:5 in my hand and Hebrews 12:2 in my heart. As far as I could tell the only ground I had given Satan was in my introspection. I had taken my eyes off the sufficiency of Christ for a moment and put them on my performance. I know better than this, and for years I have faithfully preached the unsearchable riches of Christ. I learned a new depth to an old truth. Soldier of Christ, regardless of your age or station be careful to always keep your big gun clean and ready for action at a moment's notice. The biggest gun you have in your arsenal is the glorious gospel. "Looking unto Jesus the author and finisher of our faith; who for the joy that was set before him endured the cross, despising the shame, and is set down at the right hand of the throne of God" (Heb. 12:2)

No More Powerful Weapon Than the Gospel

After a few more moments of singing and praising the Lord for His goodness, He led me to 1 Peter where He was about to give me another new depth to an old truth. "Forasmuch as ye know that ye were not redeemed with corruptible things, like silver and gold, from your vain manner of life received by tradition from your fathers; but with the precious blood of Christ, as of a lamb without blemish and without spot" (1 Pet. 1:18–19). I have had those verses committed to memory for many years and have quoted them often during sermons but a new depth of appreciation came: <u>without blemish</u>. The only acceptable sacrifice to God the Father is God the Son because He is the only offering that is without blemish. It is not the sincerity of my faith nor the purity of my motives. It is not my tears of repentance nor how genuine my sorrow is over sin. It is not the steadfastness of my service nor the fineness of my theology. Every offering, every sacrifice I make to God, other than through Jesus, has some pollutant in it. All of my so called virtue and chasteness, uprightness and morality have blemishes in them because there is too much of me in the offering. It is not my self-denials or disciplines; not my sacrificial giving or even the multitude of sermons I've preached which I offer to God for my salvation. I am convinced that I have never preached a sermon that is without blemish. Oh, how I would hate to have something that I have done be the hope of my salvation.

Taking the Shield of Faith

I took hold of the Sword of the Spirit once again and passionately quoted, "[God] hath saved us, and called us with a holy calling, not according to our works, but according to his own purpose and grace, which was given us in Christ Jesus before the world began, but is now made manifest by the appearing of our Savior Jesus Christ, who hath abolished death, and brought life and immortality to light through the gospel" (2 Tim. 1:9–10). I thank God for doctors, but I got carried away in thanking God even more for Jesus, the Great Physician who has abolished death and brought eternal life through the gospel. No earthly doctor has abolished death. We must preach the "blemish-less' sacrifice of Christ alone as our only hope of redemption. "For we preach not ourselves, but Christ Jesus the Lord, and ourselves your servants for Jesus' sake" (2 Cor. 4:5). I began to sing praise to God and recalled a verse from a great hymn, "Before the Throne of God Above":

When Satan tempts me to despair,
And tells me of the guilt within,
Upward I look, and see Him there
Who made an end to all my sin.

Because the sinless Savior died,
My sinful soul is counted free;
For God the just is satisfied
To look on Him and pardon me
To look on Him and pardon me

If your faith is not in the Christ of the gospel, you have no shield to protect you from Satan's accusations. If your faith is in the gospel then you must become good at using it as a weapon when the enemy of your soul tempts you to take your eyes off Christ.

BACK TO MORE GOSPEL

Within a few moments, I was drawn to the cross of Calvary; more specifically to the repentant thief on the cross next to Jesus. Jesus was crucified between two thieves and both of them heard the jeers and mocking from the crowd. Little did they know they were hearing elements of the gospel while seeing Christ's compassion for others. They heard people saying that Jesus claimed to be the Son of God; that He was the Christ, the promised Savior. The inscription above His head was written in three languages—"This is Jesus, the King of the Jews." One of the first things they would have heard Jesus say as the soldiers dropped His cross in its hole was, "Father, forgive them for they know not what they do." They observed the compassion He had toward His mother. They heard the caring discourse and charge of responsibility He gave young John on her behalf. Let's go to the gospel of Luke chapter 23 for further details of how the two thieves responded to the Person and work of Christ.

Two very similar men hearing the same things, in the same situation, respond very differently. "And one of the malefactors who were hanged railed at him, saying, If thou be the Christ, save thyself and us" (v. 39). It is obvious from this statement that he had no faith in anything beyond this life. For him it was only the here and now. What a sad state of affairs to live only by sight in the temporary self-centered concerns of this world alone. "But the other answering rebuked him, saying, Dost thou not fear God, seeing thou art in the same condemnation? And we indeed justly; for we receive the due reward of our deeds. But this man hath done nothing amiss" (vv. 40–41). Only by the grace of God did this man realize the very world was being judged on the cross of Jesus. The fear of one day standing before God, the righteous Judge of all the earth, gripped his soul. In that moment he realized his condemned state and his desperate need for mercy. He confessed that he deserved justice for the crimes he had committed. But more so by the grace of God, he knew he needed a cleansing of the sinful heart from which those actions had come. These two malefactors were called thieves in Matthew's account. They weren't petty thieves, pickpockets or shoplifters. These men were the kind of thieves who beat you to death and left you bleeding and dying along some remote stretch of highway, similar to the story of the man who fell among thieves on the Jericho road (see Lu. 10:30–37). It would be easy to point to them and say their crime was a capital offense; but not mine. I've not done anything as bad as them. According to Scripture, one bite of one piece of forbidden fruit places me under the same condemnation as Adam. By the grace of God this second thief was feeling the weight of his sinful nature, not just the crimes for which he had been caught.

By the grace of God he also realized that Jesus was absolutely innocent. There was no blemish in Him. Could this Jesus be the promised Messiah the Savior of the world? Could this be the Lamb of God whose blood would wash away his sin, give him forgiveness, and grant him life beyond the grave? I believe he understood the gospel when he helplessly looked at Jesus as if to humbly say, "There is nothing I can do for you, but there is something you can do for me." The glory of the gospel is not something we do for God, but what He has done for us. The gospel is God's doing. I had nothing to do with it. God alone authored it and He alone perfected it. The gospel is about what God has done for man. The thief got it when he said there is something you can do for me, "Remember me when thou comest into thy kingdom" (v. 42). There is a future life beyond the kingdom of this world. One day the kingdoms of this world will become the kingdom of our God and of His Christ and He shall reign forever and ever.

I love the response of Jesus: He didn't ask him what he had done to get in such a fix. He didn't ask him if he had been circumcised, if he smoked or drank. He didn't ask him when was the last time he had been to a service at the synagogue. He didn't ask him any questions on his lineage or the kind of home he had grown up in. He didn't ask him if he were a Pharisee or a Sadducee, a Democrat or a Republican. He just looked at him and said, "Today shalt thou be with me in paradise (v. 43). This man who all his life had been dead in his trespasses and sins was in that instant made spiritually alive. Oh, the blessedness of passing from death to life before it is too late. Right to the end of His life Jesus was saving people who looked to Him alone for salvation. He continues to do the same today. If you understand the gospel message, then confess yourself a sinner and believe in your heart that what He has done for you, not what you could ever do for Him, is your only hope of eternal life. He will save you.

Getting Good With Your Weapon

This Christian soldier is always better for having fought in the battle. After the attack of the enemy, my sword had been honed on the stone and was much sharper than before. Good soldiers are not made in a school. They do not become battle hardened by sitting in class listening to lectures. I learned more in one week on the road as a Michigan State Trooper than I did in three months in the academy. Fight the good fight of faith, do the job of defending what you believe when the enemy of your soul casts doubts on the sufficiency of Christ and the gospel.

When I joined the police department I had never handled a hand gun before. I had a terrible time learning the use of it but eventually I qualified as a Sharpshooter, the lowest score possible to still qualify for the job. Every year we had to qualify with our weapon. We could improve our status if we improved our score. In about two years I moved from Sharpshooter to Marksman. I would go to the range and practice. I would shoot with the right hand and the left hand. I shot while standing and while kneeling behind barricades. I shot fast and I shot slow. I would even practice my quick draw. The more I practiced the more proficient I became. The more proficient I became the more confident I became. In another two years I went from Marksman to Expert and eventually in another year I went from Expert to Distinguished Expert. Through much practice I had gone from the lowest status to the highest. It is the same way with the gospel: it is your weapon against the enemy of your soul. When he tempts you to doubt the sufficiency of Christ your biggest gun is the gospel. Know what it is and what it is not and practice so you will be prepared and confident when you need to use it.

The Gospel Is Not

The gospel is not
confession, repentance, obedience, or worship.
The gospel is not
church, missions, discipleship or baptism.
The gospel is not
prayer, faith, commitment, or surrender.
The gospel is not
election, predestination, foreknowledge, or sovereignty.
The gospel is not
a sect, a creed, a catechism, or sacraments.
The gospel is not
a day, a duty, a denomination or a religion.
The gospel is not
Apollos or Paul, Calvin or Wesley, Luther or Knox.
The gospel is not
a dispensation, cessation, or reformation.
The gospel is not
pre-trib, mid-trib, post-trib, or a-trib.
The gospel is not
my discipline or my self-denial.
The gospel is not
my believing or my receiving.

The Gospel Is

The gospel is the declaration of God's love demonstrated when He offered His only Son as a sacrifice for sin which He did by Himself, in Himself, for Himself—so that He would be glorified in redeeming all who would hear and believe, (see 1 Cor. 15:1–4, Col. 1:20–23, Rom. 10:9–10, and 1 Pet. 3:18).

The gospel is not salvation; salvation is what occurs when the gospel is believed. The gospel is the gospel whether we believe it or not.

The gospel is not about taking a good man, mixing in a little religious behavior and making him a better man. The gospel is taking a man who is spiritually dead and giving him life. "And you hath he made alive, who were dead in trespasses and sins" (Eph. 2:1). The gospel is about taking a man who has been born spiritually blind and giving him sight. The gospel is about taking a man who has been legitimately convicted and sentenced to life in prison and setting him free. Jesus made this clear as He stood and read the Scriptures in the synagogue of Nazareth. "The Spirit of the Lord is upon me, because he hath anointed me to preach the gospel to the poor; he hath sent me to heal the brokenhearted, to preach deliverance to the captives, and recovering of sight to the blind, to set at liberty them that are bruised" (Lu. 4:18).

BLESSED ASSURANCE

As we have traveled preaching the gospel, we have spoken with so many fine believers who struggle with doubts of their salvation. Most only need to hear the simple truths of the gospel to have their faith strengthened, their peace returned, and their confidence increased. If we lower our eyes from the cross and look at our performance we will begin to doubt; but if we keep looking unto Jesus the Author and Finisher of our faith we will stand fast in the faith. "Let us hold fast the profession of our faith without wavering (for faithful is he that promised)" (Heb. 10:23). The profession of our faith is vital to our stand against the devil. Far too many believers cannot articulate the gospel. They haven't taken the time to become good with this powerful weapon. Every believer should make it his aim to memorize certain gospel verses. Here are just a few to get you started: 1 Cor. 15:1–4, Rom. 3:24–26, John 3:16, 2 Tim. 1:9–10, Eph. 2:8–9, Heb. 6:18–20, and Acts 4:12.

Oh, Christian soldier, if the prince of darkness points out your failures to get you to focus on them, take your stand and say, "My performance is not my hope of salvation. God's performance in Christ alone is my hope of salvation." Preach the gospel to yourself; use the Scriptures. The enemy will hear it and flee in terror at the very mention of what occurred at Calvary. The cross was Satan's undoing and our triumph over all the wicked spirits in league with him. "And you being dead in your sins and the uncircumcision of your flesh, hath he made alive together with him, having forgiven you all trespasses, blotting out the handwriting of ordinances that was against us, and took it out of the way, nailing it to his cross; and having spoiled principalities and powers, he made a show of them openly, triumphing over them in it" (Col. 2:13–15). The cross is where Jesus made a public display of the enemy's defeat sealing his eventual doom in the lake of fire.

I encourage people to be serious about knowing the gospel and using it as a big gun against Satan's accusations, to enter the battle prepared to stand. The more you use your weapon, the better you will get with it. The better you get with it, the more assurance you will have in your ability to use it. My favorite hymn is "Blessed Assurance."

Blessed assurance Jesus is mine!
O, what a foretaste of glory divine!
Heir of salvation, purchase of God,
Born of his Spirit, washed in his blood.

The battle has made me better and I thank God for using Satan to remind me of how much I need Christ. The gospel continues to become more glorious to me. That is a good thing in developing endurance as a good soldier of Jesus Christ.

CHAPTER FIVE

ADDING TO YOUR ARSENAL

A good soldier is one who is trained in the use of more than one weapon. In Bible times, the Roman soldier would become skilled in the use of the bow and arrow, spear, dagger, and sword. The kind of weapon he would use depended a lot on the type of enemy he faced and the terrain of the battle. The Christian solder doesn't always get to choose the time and terrain of battle so he must be prepared for anything. Satan loves the element of surprise and uses it to his advantage. No wonder Paul encouraged the Church to always be on their guard, dressed and ready for battle. "See then that ye walk circumspectly, not as fools, but as wise, redeeming the time, because the days are evil" (Eph. 5:15–16).

In my morning prayers I include a list of weapons I take with me to the battle. All of these weapons are good weapons. The more I learn how to use them the more victorious I become. In this chapter I will list them, give the reasons I chose them, and how I use them. This is not intended to be an exhaustive list but one that is serving me well at this time and place in my journey of faith.

The Sword of the Spirit

The sword of the Spirit is defined in Scripture as the Word of God. "And [take] the sword of the Spirit, which is the word of God" (Eph. 6:17b). When Jesus was in the wilderness, the place where the enemy always likes to find us, Jesus used Old Testament Scripture to respond to the enemy's assault. Three temptations were shot at Him and three times He responded, "It is written." Jesus always answered with what was already written in the Word of Scripture. Our Great Example didn't have to quote verses which were already written for He was in fact the Word of God Himself. He could have done something supernatural like turn the stones into bread, but He knew we couldn't, so He did what He knew we could do. He quoted the Scripture. When the enemy assaults you with some kind of temptation, always resist him with Scripture; he will soon weaken and flee if you stand your ground.

A Plug for Scripture Memory

Scripture memory is not an option if one is to win in a spiritual battle. Scripture memory has been a life changer for me and has made the difference between victory and defeat. "For we wrestle not against flesh and blood, but against principalities, against powers, against the rulers of the darkness of this world, against spiritual wickedness in high places" (Eph. 6:12). As a Christian you know something of the reality of this battle. As a soldier with armor and weapons, you know you can't just ignore the enemy and hope he goes away. Determine to know some Scripture by memory and have it ready for when you come under attack. You don't have to memorize a lot of Scripture, but you should memorize a few verses well.

The devil is a student of human behavior. He knows where you are most vulnerable to attack. If you have struggled with unforgiveness and bitterness, he loves to remind you of the wrongs you have suffered. You would do well to have Eph. 4:32 and Col. 3:13 committed to memory. Study and meditate on the power of these verses and when the enemy tries to gain the ground in that area, quote them either to yourself or aloud , if you feel the occasion requires it. Forgiveness is not easy; but the only thing I know that is harder than forgiveness is unforgiveness. Satan will destroy us if we do not forgive others. "To whom ye forgive anything, I forgive also; for if I forgave anything, to whom I forgave it, for your sakes forgave I it in the person of Christ, lest Satan should get an advantage of us; for we are not ignorant of his devices" (2 Cor. 2:10–11). It is important to know that forgiveness is not a feeling. It is obedience to objective truth. Don't live by your feelings for on many occasions they have proven themselves to be unreliable; live by your faith. "For the word of God is living, and powerful, and sharper than any two-edged sword, piercing even to the dividing asunder of soul and spirit, and of the joints and marrow, and is a discerner of the thoughts and intents of the heart" (Heb. 4:12). If you hide God's Word in your heart it will keep you from sin. Sin is what the devil capitalizes on. If you give him an inch, before you know it he quickly becomes a ruler.

This same principle applies to a host of other areas. It could be anger, wrath, lust, greed, covetousness or any number of sins. Most of us have an area of vulnerability. We would be wise to prepare for battle with the Sword in hand. Me and my words are no match for Satan, but Satan is no match for God and His Words.

The Powerful Hand of Prayer

When taking up my weapons in my morning prayers, I always start by praying these words, "I take the Sword of the Spirit, which is the Word of God, grasping it tightly with the powerful hand of prayer." Prayer is the soldier's greatest expression of faith. He is never more powerful than when he is praying. Prayer is our direct contact with the Commander and Chief. It is access to the One and only Almighty God. "Therefore being justified by faith, we have peace with God through our Lord Jesus Christ: by whom also we have access by faith into this grace in which we stand, and rejoice in hope of the glory of God" (Rom. 5:1–2). We are to pray without ceasing. "Be anxious for nothing; but in everything by prayer and supplication with thanksgiving let your requests be made known unto God" (Phil. 4:6). Worry about nothing, pray about everything, and be thankful for anything. When the battle is raging all around you, determine never to panic, but always to pray. Prayer is your battle cry to heaven and it will not go unheard.

John 17 records the prayer of Jesus for His disciples. In that prayer he prayed for their protection from the evil one. "I pray not that thou shouldest take them out of the world, but that thou shouldest keep them from the evil" (v. 15). He prayed that the Father wouldn't take them out of the world. When you are in heaven you are beyond the devil's reach, but not here. To be left on earth to fight the good fight is a blessed opportunity to live by faith. Jesus made it clear that He wanted them to have the privilege of being soldiers. He just wanted the Father to keep them or protect them from the plans of the evil one.

I regularly ask God to deny Satan any permission to do anything against me or my family. Satan was considering God's servant Job, just hoping for the permission to assault him. I wonder how many things my family and I have escaped just because of prayer. "There hath no temptation taken you but such as is common to man; but God is faithful, who will not permit you to be tempted above that ye are able, but will with the temptation also make a way of escape, that ye may be able to bear it" (1 Cor. 10:13).

There are times that I pray for God to send holy warring angels to do the work of the ministry that I cannot do. When surrounded by the enemy, the prophet Elisha knew if God were for him it didn't matter who was against him. His servant could only see the enemy and was terrified. Elisha calmly said that the odds were in their favor for there were more with them than there was with the enemy. "And he answered, Fear not; for they who are with us are more than they who are with them. And Elisha prayed, and said, Lord, I pray thee, open his eyes, that he may see. And the Lord opened the eyes of the young man, and he saw; and, behold, the mountain was full of horses and chariots of fire round about Elisha" (2 Ki. 6:16–17).

I believe prayer is often a contest between angels who minister and demons that hinder. Yes, Satan can hinder the saint in his journey. "Wherefore we would have come unto you, even I Paul, once and again; but Satan hindered us" (1 Thess. 2:18). The admonition of Scripture remains the same. "Call unto me, and I will answer thee, and show thee great and mighty things, which thou knowest not' (Jer. 33:3). Pray all kinds of prayers at all kinds of times, about all kinds of things; pray *for* things, and *against* things but by all means pray. "Praying always with all prayer and supplication in the Sprit, and watching thereunto with all perseverance and supplication for all saints" (Eph. 6:18).

IN THE NAME

When the seventy returned from their first ministry tour, the first thing they said was that even the demons were subject to them in His name, (see Lu 10:17). God never said not to use His Name; He just said not to use it in vain. We pray in His Name, we baptize in His Name, we preach in His Name and in His Name have authority to command evil spirits to leave and take their wicked works with them. "And it came to pass, as we went to prayer, a certain maid possessed with a spirit of divination met us, who brought her masters much gain by soothsaying. The same followed Paul and us, and cried, saying, These men are the servants of the most high God, who show unto us the way of salvation. And this she did many days. But Paul, being grieved, turned and said to the spirit, I command thee in the name of Jesus Christ to come out of her. And he came out the same hour" (Acts 16:16–18).

On my web page there is a list of names, titles and attributes of Him who is Lord of all; but there is one Name that tops them all and that is the Name Jesus. "Wherefore, God also hath highly exalted him, and given him a name which is above every name: that at the name of Jesus every knee should bow, of things in heaven, and things in earth, and things under the earth, and that every tongue should confess that Jesus Christ is Lord, to the glory of God the Father" (Phil. 2:9–11).

The Name of Jesus is the Christian soldier's badge of authority. When I was in the State Police there were times when I would have to execute search warrants or arrest warrants. Usually several officers were present but only one would knock on the door. When the voice on the other side asked who it was, I never said, "Open up in the name of Tom Harmon." I would never use my name; my name had no authority at all. I would say, "State Police, open up." If they weren't complying within a few seconds and we heard sounds like getting rid of evidence, we had the legal authority to kick in the door and serve the warrants. We had the authority of the State Legislature behind us. When you have the people who make the laws behind you, you have all the authority you need. God Himself is the entire judicial system. He gives us, as His children, the right to use His Name. Use it reverently for it is a worthy Name by which we are called.

In the late 1700's Edward Perronet penned a great hymn for the church, "All Hail the Power of Jesus' Name."

All hail the power of Jesus' Name! Let angels prostrate fall;
Bring forth the royal diadem, and crown Him Lord of all.
Bring forth the royal diadem, and crown Him Lord of all.

Jesus is the Name of the One who is King of Kings and Lord of Lords.

The Precious Blood

God required a blood sacrifice for the sin of Adam and Eve. A sacrifice He, Himself, carried out by offering innocent animals. Their blood made atonement for Adam and Eve. From Adam all the way to Moses, God made it clear that without the shedding of blood there would be no remission of sin. At the first Passover, before the Exodus, if God did not see the blood on the lintel and doorpost of the home, the firstborn of that household would die. All the blood of the animal sacrifices made by the Jews over the centuries could never accomplish what the blood of Christ did at Calvary. "Neither by the blood of goats and calves, but by his own blood he entered in once into the holy place, having obtained eternal redemption for us" (Heb. 9:12).

God came to earth in the person of His Son to shed his blood on the cross as a payment for the penalty of man's sin. The power of this event would affect the entire world. When John the Baptist saw Jesus coming down the road he spoke to his disciples and said, "Behold the Lamb of God, who taketh away the sin of the world" (John 1:29b). The Jews knew the significance of a perfect lamb for the sacrifice of their sin; it had to be one without blemish and without spot. Jesus alone met all the qualifications that God demanded. His blood alone could cleanse man from his sin and destroy the works of the devil. "And he is the propitiation for our sins: and not for ours only, but also for the sins of the whole world" (1 John 2:2). "Unto him who loved us and washed us from our sins in his own blood" (Rev. 1:5b).

Satan would have loved to have seen Jesus thrown over a cliff, hung by the neck or drown in the sea; anything but have His blood shed on the cross. Satan must have turned pale as he understood what it meant. Satan's doom was sealed and his works destroyed. "For this purpose the Son of God was manifested, that he might destroy the works of the devil" (1 John 3:8b). Use the overcoming power of the blood of Christ in your statement of faith against the lies and temptations of the devil. "And they overcame [the accuser] by the blood of the Lamb, and by the word of their testimony; and they loved not their lives unto the death" (Rev. 12:11).

My hope is built on nothing less
than Jesus' blood and righteousness.

Redeemed, how I love to proclaim it!
Redeemed by the blood of the Lamb;
Redeemed thro' His infinite mercy,
His child and forever I am.

What can wash away my sin?
Nothing but the blood of Jesus;
What can make me whole again?
Nothing but the blood of Jesus.

PRAISING

In 2 Chronicles chapter 20 is recorded the moving account of King Jehoshaphat and how the Lord delivered him from his enemies. He sought the Lord in humility and God gave him the weapon of praise to take to the battle. The conclusion of the story goes like this, "And they rose early in the morning, and went forth into the wilderness of Tekoa: and as they went forth, Jehoshaphat stood and said, Hear me, O Judah, and ye inhabitants of Jerusalem; Believe in the Lord your God, so shall ye be established; believe his prophets, so shall ye prosper. And when he had consulted with the people, he appointed singers unto the Lord, who should praise the beauty of holiness, as they went out before the army, and to say, Praise the Lord; for his mercy endureth forever. And when they began to sing, and to praise, the Lord set an ambush against the children of Ammon, Moab, and Mount Seir, who were come against Judah; and they were smitten" (vv. 20:20–22).

King David was a mighty warrior. His victories far outnumbered his defeats. He knew of the spiritual battles that he and his people faced. No other Bible writer speaks more on the subject of praise. He knew the power of praising the Lord and its effect on the kingdom of darkness.

"I will bless the Lord at all times;
his praise shall continually be in my mouth.
My soul shall make her boast in the Lord;
the humble shall hear of it and be glad.
Oh magnify the Lord with me,
and let us exalt his name together.
I sought the Lord, and he heard me,
and delivered me from all my fears.

The angel of the Lord encampeth round about those who
fear him and delivereth them."
(Psa. 34:1–4,7)

"Oh that men would praise the Lord for his goodness, and
for his wonderful works to the children of men!
(Psa. 107:8,15,21,31)

It is my custom to spend a few moments at the beginning of
each day just praising the Lord. I have often wondered how
many of the enemy's plans were thwarted before they ever had
a chance to develop just because of this practice. "To the praise
of the glory of his grace, through which he hath made us accepted in the beloved" (Eph. 1:6). "By him, therefore let us
offer the sacrifice of praise to God continually, that is, the fruit
of our lips giving thanks to his name" (Heb. 13:15). Praise is
always appropriate. Do it before the battle and you may not
have to fight; do it during the battle and you might not have
to fight so long; do it after the battle and you will clean up any
residue lingering around after the fight.

PERSEVERING

Napoleon was once asked what made a good soldier. His reply was quick and clear. "Perseverance," he said. It's not always the one with skill on the battlefield who wins, but the one who can endure the hardships and privations of military life. The soldier who can endure short rations, cold nights, long marches, and still show up ready to fight the battle, will win. Perseverance is the mark of a good soldier.

The Christian soldier is called to endure hardship and persevere in the face of a relentless unseen foe. Satan never takes a day off, not even Sundays. We are called to be on guard and ever alert to danger. "Ye therefore, beloved, seeing ye know these things before, beware lest ye also, being led away with the error of the wicked, fall from your own steadfastness" (2 Pet. 3:17). Every soldier needs to have his heart fixed on the goal of finishing well, of dying in the midst of the battle, not as a spectator on the sidelines. This is surely what was intended when Paul wrote, "Wherefore take unto you the whole armor of God that ye may be able to withstand in the evil day, and having done all, to stand. Stand, therefore...." (Eph. 6:13–14). One would have to be in total denial to say that evil days never come. The question is, will I stand strong in the Lord and the power of His might? "From that time many of his disciples went back, and walked no more with him. Then said Jesus unto the twelve, Will you also go away? Then Simon Peter answered him, Lord, to whom shall we go? Thou hast the words of eternal life. And we believe and are sure that thou art the Christ, the Son of the living God" (John 6:66–69). You can be sure that days of adversity will come. "If thou faint in the day of adversity, thy strength is small" (Prov. 24:10).

"Blessed is the man that endureth temptation; for when he is tried, he shall receive the crown of life, which the Lord hath promised to them that love him" (Jas. 1:12). Perseverance belongs to the one who sees beyond the battles to the ultimate victory of eternity. "Looking unto Jesus the author and finisher of our faith; who for the joy that was set before him endured the cross, despising the shame, and is set down at the right hand of the throne of God. For consider him that endured such contradiction of sinners against himself, lest ye be wearied and faint in your minds" (Heb. 12:2–3).

SEEKING GODLY COMRADES

There are times when we are left all alone, even friends desert us. This is when the enemy likes to come in like a flood and make sore hash out of us. Jesus was alone in the wilderness when He faced Satan's worst. When the Apostle Paul was alone in Athens, he sent immediately for Silas and Timothy knowing they would add strength and encouragement to his soul. He recalled one time when no one stood with him and he could literally feel Satan's breath he was so near. "At my first defense no man stood with me, but all men forsook me; I pray God that it may not be laid to their charge. Notwithstanding, the Lord stood with me and strengthened me; that by me the preaching might be fully known, and that all the Gentiles might hear. And I was delivered out of the mouth of the lion. And the Lord shall deliver me from every evil work, and will preserve me unto his heavenly kingdom: to whom be glory forever and ever. Amen" (2 Tim. 4:16–18).

The devil loves to catch some wandering sheep all alone. Don't be a loner, it's dangerous. The Apostle Paul sought godly comrades. He had Silas, Timothy, Luke, Epaphras, John Mark and others who helped him in the gospel ministry. I am by nature independent and enjoy being alone. I have learned that you can be alone to a fault. I asked God to send some godly, low maintenance, praying friends into my life and He has. I thank God for allowing me to see the value of godly comrades. They have been a great help in my spiritual battles.

BY THE WORD OF OUR TESTIMONY

Always be ready to give a testimony to the things God is doing in your life. We are to be witnesses of the good things He has done for us. "But sanctify the Lord God in your hearts: and be ready always to give an answer to every man that asketh you a reason of the hope that is in you with meekness and fear" (1 Pet. 3:15).

I led a men's discipleship group for seven years; it was called "Faithful Men of Michigan." It was based on 2 Timothy 2:2. One of the assignments was that each man had to write out his salvation testimony and eventually share it with the group. It didn't have to be long but it did have to include something about their life before they came to Christ, how they came to Christ and how the gospel had changed their life. For some of the men this was the first time they had ever given public testimony to their faith. To a man, it helped their faith! It was good for the man who bore testimony as well as the men who heard it. I am convinced that anything that strengthens a man's faith weakens the effect the kingdom of darkness has on him.

Bear testimony in your home and especially to your children. If one generation stops telling the next generation about their faith, there will be a generation who doesn't know about God. "And also all that generation were gathered unto their fathers; and there arose another generation after them, who knew not the Lord, nor yet the works which he had done for Israel. And the children of Israel did evil in the sight of the Lord, and served Baalim" (Judg. 2:10–11). Baalim or Baal was the common name for the Canaanites' god. One of their favorite names for Baal was Baal-Zebub meaning Lord of the flies or the prince of demons. When we do not bear testimony to those God has placed within our sphere of influence we leave them vulnerable to the deceptive powers of the devil. Verbalize your faith; it is a powerful weapon against the devil.

Amazing Grace

Grace is the God-given enabling power by which we do all the things the Lord has commanded us to do. God will never call us to do anything that He will not enable us to accomplish. "And God is able to make all grace abound toward you, that ye, always having all sufficiency in all things, may abound to every good work" (2 Cor. 9:8). The Apostle Paul gave all the credit to the grace of God for accomplishing in him all that he accomplished. "But by the grace of God I am what I am; and his grace which was given unto me, was not in vain; but I labored more abundantly than they all; yet not I, but the grace of God which was with me" (1 Cor. 15:10).

Let's say you are under attack from the enemy. You know it, his temptations to sin seem relentless and they are beginning to wear your defenses down. Maybe you have fallen into sin; now his accusations and lies are causing you to doubt all the things you know to be true about God. If I could encourage you to do one thing it would be to come to the throne of grace and cry out for mercy and help in your time of need. "Let us therefore come boldly unto the throne of grace, that we may obtain mercy, and find grace to help in time of need" (Heb. 4:16).

We are saved by grace through faith and we are to live by grace through faith. If we live a life of dependence on His grace then He gets all the glory and we get all the good. "That no flesh should glory in his presence. But of him are ye in Christ Jesus, who of God is made unto us wisdom, and righteousness, and sanctification, and redemption: that, according as it is written, He that glorieth, let him glory in the Lord" (1 Cor. 1:29–31).

There are times we need more grace than what we have on hand. I have seen Christians go through great difficulties and terrible loss yet with such confidence and peace. I couldn't imagine handling the same situation as well. I came to understand that they had grace I didn't have, and quite frankly, didn't need at that time. He gives us grace to help in time of need. God didn't create us to be independent from Him, as the devil has suggested, but instead to be totally dependent on Him. Asking for grace is not an imposition on God. "But he giveth more grace. Wherefore he saith, God resisteth the proud, but giveth grace unto the humble. Submit yourselves therefore to God. Resist the devil, and he will flee from you" (Jas. 4:6–7). A humble prayer to God for grace may be the very weapon you need to put the devil in retreat.

FASTING

In what is known as the Sermon on the Mount; recorded in Matthew 5–7, Jesus taught about doing things in secret. What is done for God when nobody is looking is the best evidence of faith. Jesus tells people not to make a show of their giving. Don't even let your left hand know what your right hand is doing; be as discreet as you can when giving your offering to the Lord. When you pray, don't make a big show of your long prayers before men, but rather go into your closet and pray to your Father in secret and your Father who sees in secret will reward you openly. When He comes to fasting it is the same thing, do it as secretly as you can and God will honor it. "Moreover when you fast, be not, as the hypocrites, of a sad countenance; for they disfigure their faces, that they may appear unto man to fast. Verily I say unto you, They have their reward. But thou, when thou fastest, anoint thine head, and wash thy face; that thou appear not unto men to fast, but unto thy Father, who is in secret; and thy Father who seeth in secret, shall reward thee openly" (Mt. 6:16–18).

Fasting is self-denial. It may be the denial of food, water or some other necessity or comfort. Learning to say no to self-weakens the old man and strengthens the new man. You may want to seriously consider fasting if you are anticipating spiritual warfare either in your own life or in another's, especially if you will be interceding for someone who is suspected of having demonic problems. More often than not when fasting is mentioned in Scripture, prayer is mentioned also. Prayer and fasting always seem to go together.

A man brought his child to Jesus and asked Him to help his child for he believed his child has an unclean spirit. He mentioned that he had brought him to the disciples but they couldn't help the child. Jesus rebuked the foul spirit and the child was made well. "And when he was come into the house, his disciples asked him privately, why could not we cast him out? And he said unto them, this kind can come forth by nothing, but by prayer and fasting" (Mk 9:28–29).

HUMILITY

The devil will take the slightest measure of pride in a man and drive him into the worst of the wilderness. Every proud man is his own idol. The slightest discontent will send him into a frenzy of saying that he deserves to be treated better than this. On the other hand, it is impossible to offend a humble man. He has already learned the key to conflict resolution: humble yourself and give up your rights. I wonder if this is what God saw in Abraham. "And Abram said unto Lot, Let there be no strife, I pray thee, between me and thee, and between my herdsmen and thy herdsmen; for we are brethren. Is not the whole land before thee? Separate thyself, I pray thee, from me: if thou wilt take the left hand, then I will go to the right; or if thou depart to the right hand, then I will go to the left" (Gen. 13:8–9). Lot chose the well-watered plains where the grazing was good and the cities for commerce were near. Abraham retreated to the mountainous Judean wilderness that was only good for grazing about three months of the year. Lot died in shame after fathering two children by his own daughters. Abraham became the father of faith and the father of many nations. "For whosoever exalteth himself shall be abased; and he that humbleth himself shall be exalted" (Lu. 14:11).

One prayer I never pray is for God to humble me. God can humble us but he gives us the option to humble ourselves. If we don't he will. If God has plans to use you, know this, he will not use a proud person. Peter was proud. After all wasn't he the one who got out of the boat and walked on the water with Jesus? When Jesus told him he would deny Him three times before the rooster crowed, Peter corrected Him and said he would die first, he would go to prison, but he would never deny his Lord. It wasn't long after he heard the rooster crow and, oh, how he was humbled. In Peter's first epistle, he mentions the importance of that lesson, "In like manner, ye younger, submit yourselves unto the elder. Yea, all of you be subject one to another, and be clothed with humility: for God resisteth the proud, and giveth grace to the humble. Humble yourselves therefore, under the mighty hand of God, that he may exalt you in due time" (1 Pet. 5:5–6). The humble man may have Satan to oppose him, but the proud man is in a much worse state. The proud man has God to oppose him.

CHAPTER SIX

A Fully Loaded Clip

A firearm is only good as long as there is ammunition in it. If you have an automatic rifle and the clip is empty, you might be able to use it as a club, but that's not very effective when facing an ambush. For the remainder of our weapons, I think it would be appropriate for us to consider them as rounds of ammunition. From what I've seen in war movies, when you are in a firefight, you don't want to run out of bullets.

A Clear Conscience

The dictionary definition of a human conscience is: "internal or self-knowledge of right or wrong; or the faculty, power or principle within us, which decides on the lawfulness or unlawfulness of our actions or affections, and instantly approves or condemns them." It is that faculty of our original nature which gives us a moral sensitivity. Everyone has a conscience whether they are saved or lost. A healthy conscience is a valuable thing in our battle with the devil. When a person violates his conscience often enough, he hardens it until he finds himself doing things he at one time would never have imagined. "Now the Spirit speaketh expressly, that in the latter times some shall depart from the faith, giving heed to seducing spirits, and doctrines of demons; speaking lies in hypocrisy; having their conscience seared with a hot iron" (1 Tim. 4:1–2). We heat our house with a free-standing cast iron wood burning stove. On one occasion I was stoking it when I hit my wrist against the very hot opening. It cauterized my skin instantly. In the days that followed I noticed the burned area had no feeling. It was not sensitive to hot, cold, nor even touch. Over time it healed and thankfully the feeling returned. A person who has lost feeling in some part of their body is vulnerable to further and worse injury. I have had times in my life when I have seared my conscience. At those times I was without the valuable protection it gives against evil and the evil one. It was a wonderful thing when the feeling returned.

When the Apostle Paul sent young Timothy to the churches of Asia to set them in order he gave him this instruction: "Now the end of the commandment is love out of a pure heart, and of a good conscience, and of faith unfeigned" (1 Tim. 1:5). Paul stressed the importance of these goals again in just a few verses later when writing on spiritual warfare. "This charge I commit unto thee, son Timothy, according to the prophecies which pointed to thee, that thou by them mightiest war a good warfare; holding faith, and a good conscience; which some having put away concerning faith have made a shipwreck" (1 Tim. 1:18–19). A few verses later he mentions it yet again. "Holding the mystery of the faith in a pure conscience" (1 Tim. 3:9). Paul seemed to be more concerned about Timothy's conscience than his faith. He knew Timothy had a good grip on the faith and would keep the faith. He also knew the danger of compromising one's conscience. Satan will take advantage of every little compromise of the conscience. The old adage, "let your conscience be your guide," would be better said, "let the Holy Spirit guide your conscience." Remember, the Holy Spirit is not the only spirit that speaks to our conscience. "In which in times past ye walked according to the course of this world, according to the prince of the power of the air, the spirit that now worketh in the sons of disobedience" (Eph. 2:2).

MORAL PURITY

Speaking of a behavior as being either moral or immoral makes direct reference to the law of God as the standard by which a person's actions are judged. There is no standard of right or wrong behavior, no code of ethics, if there is no judge to bring to account. The word "moral" speaks volumes about the holy, righteous standard of God by which He will one day judge all men. When an action is said to be morally pure, it means it lines up with the righteous standard of God. Morality covers a lot of ground and speaks to a number of issues, but more often than not, it references sexual behavior. Sexual purity is the focus of this armament.

Few are the men who have not struggled in the sphere of sexual purity. Struggling with sexual purity is not unique to men but I write from a man's perspective; a man who has known both victory and defeat. I must write candidly about the importance of this subject. I have a message I have preached many times, the title of which is, "All of the Greats." All of the great saints in the sermon had one thing in common: they were defeated in the area of sexual purity. The strongest man who ever lived, Samson, died a broken man because of his Delilah. King David was the bravest man who ever lived. Who would ever have dreamed he would secretly take a loyal friend's wife, then subtly plot his death? Solomon, the wisest man that ever lived, died a babbling old fool worshiping idols in the temple of his foreign wives. God was not pleased with him. Judah, the patriarch of the very tribe from which the Lord Jesus came, was a very immoral man who raised immoral sons. When on the way to the sheepshearer's, he saw a woman dressed like a harlot, struck a deal with her and went on his way. She asked for a pledge of his bracelet and staff until a servant was to return with payment. He never saw her face or recognized her as his own daughter-in-law. She left for home before the servant could return and recover Judah's identifying bracelet and staff. When she, a widow, was discovered with child, she accurately identified Judah as the father. These men are not peripheral men when it comes to knowing God. These are big hitters. Satan loves when we satisfy our God-created desires in God-forbidden ways.

Purity in this area of a man's life is worth the fight. Coming to my own victory was not swift or unopposed. Let me explain that when I say victory, I don't just mean taking the high ground. Victory in this arena means taking the high ground and holding it. The enemy doesn't go away just because we take the day. He has a track record of making statistics out of even "Great Men." Victory comes from embracing this admonition. Hold tightly to the scripture of Ephesians 6:13 and having done all, stand having your loins girded about you with truth. "Let not thine heart decline to [the strange woman's] ways; go not astray in her paths. For she hath cast down many wounded: yea, many strong men have been slain by her. Her house is the way to hell, going down to the chambers of death" (Prov. 7:25–27).

Regardless of where you are in this area of your life, let me encourage you to press on to victory. A man will be more apt to invade Satan's territory with the gospel of Christ when he knows Satan no longer holds this stronghold against him.

SERVING

One thing is certain in this old life: everybody is serving somebody. For too much of my life, I was self-serving all the while ignorantly having the full approval of Satan. He doesn't care if I am committed to outright serving him. He doesn't care whom I serve as long as it keeps me from serving God. I remember coming to the place in my life when I really wanted to serve God. I was listening to a sermon from Mark 10 when I was struck with the fact that Jesus didn't come to be served but to serve. He was speaking to His self-serving disciples when He said, "And whosoever of you would be the chiefest, shall be servant of all" (v. 44). My commitment to serve the Lord was the first step in dismantling one of the strongholds Satan had in my life. It was the stronghold of greed or temporal values. "No man can serve two masters; for either he will hate the one, and love the other; or else he will hold to the one, and despise the other. Ye cannot serve God and money" (Mt. 6:24). Money in itself is amoral, but the love of it can become a cruel taskmaster. It often times does. The stronghold fell when I came to realize that everything I had belonged to God and I was but a servant, a steward of His riches.

Satan's third temptation of Christ in the wilderness was a promise to give Him all the kingdoms of the world if Jesus would fall down and worship him. "Then saith Jesus unto him, Be gone, Satan; for it is written, Thou shalt worship the Lord God, and him only shalt thou serve" (Mt. 4:10). Those clear commanding words put the boots to Satan and he left defeated. Jesus would be the Suffering Servant all the way to the cross. But then He arose from the tomb as our conquering King. "Let this mind be in you, which was also in Christ Jesus: who, being in the form of God, thought it not robbery to be equal with

God: but made himself of no reputation, and took upon him the form of a servant, and was made in the likeness of men; And being found in fashion as a man, he humbled himself, and became obedient unto death, even the death of the cross" (Phil. 2:5–8). A soldier committed to serving his King is in a win/win situation.

Good Works

Light and darkness are often used in Scripture as metaphors for good and evil. Light often refers to God and His kingdom while darkness often refers to Satan and his kingdom. "Every good gift and every perfect gift is from above, and cometh down from the Father of lights, with whom is no variableness, neither shadow of turning" (Jas. 1:17). Revelation 16:10 refers to Satan's kingdom as being full of darkness. Good works then are those which show forth light while darkness proceeds from evil works.

We are not saved by good works, but we are saved to them. "For by grace are ye saved through faith; and that not of yourselves: it is a gift of God: not of works, lest any man should boast. For we are his workmanship, created in Christ Jesus unto good works, which God hath before ordained that we should walk in them" (Eph. 2:8–10). Good works that glorify God are like a powerful light in a dark world. The rulers of darkness flee like a bunch of cockroaches when we let our light so shine before men that they glorify our Father in heaven.

Paul warned Titus about those who talked a good fight but never let their light shine in the world. The Christian life is so much easier to talk than to walk, but talk is cheap and the world knows it. Quite frankly the world is sick of our theology; it wants to see our faith. The rulers of darkness tremble when faith-based good works adorn the Christian soldier. "Unto the pure all things are pure: but unto them that are defiled and unbelieving is nothing pure; but even their mind and conscience is defiled. They profess that they know God; but in works they deny him, being abominable, and disobedient, and unto every good work reprobate" (Tit. 1:15–16). A reprobate mind is one which can no longer process truth. In such a mind darkness prevails.

The difference between sight and blindness is the same as between light and darkness. You can have 20/20 vision, but it isn't worth a biscuit without light. Paul went on further in his letter to Titus to say he needed to be a pattern of good works (v. 2:7), to have a passion for good works (v. 2:14), and to maintain a program for good works (v. 3:8). The Bible, our manual of arms, is our call to good works. Good works will equip us to fight well in the heat of battle. "That ye might be blameless and harmless, the children of God, without rebuke, in the midst of a crooked and perverse nation, among whom ye shine as lights in the world; holding forth the word of life, that I may rejoice in the day of Christ, that I have not run in vain, neither labored in vain" (Phil. 2:15–16). The works of darkness are never an asset to the soldier of light.

WORSHIP

The Christian soldier is at his very best when he is worshiping the Lord in spirit and in truth. The devil did his best to entice Jesus to worship him, but Jesus presented the truth of Scripture very clearly, "Thou shalt worship the Lord thy God and him only shalt thou serve" (Mt. 4:10b). Worship in the spirit may express itself in many ways, but it is always according to truth. The standard for truth is the Bible. Be very cautious of "worshipful experiences" which are outside the guidelines of Scripture. Be careful not to worship the act of worship. Be careful also not to worship the works of your own hands. "Their land also is full of idols; they worship the works of their own hands, that which their own fingers have made" (Isa. 2:8). Be careful of worshiping self. King Nebuchadnezzar spoke to himself and said, "Is not this great Babylon, that I have built for the house of the kingdom by the might of my power, and for the honor of my majesty?" (Dan. 4:30). True worship is a powerful thing; misguided worship is a dangerous thing.

In the early '90s I was studying the subject of worship. I read five or so great books on the subject and was deeply moved at how lacking my faith was in this commanding principle of Scripture. I was beginning to wonder if I had ever worshiped God. I began to seek the Lord and ask Him to teach me how to truly worship Him. I have learned several things over the years but I want to share just one. It is a simple truth with powerful insights to true worship. Every year I choose a goal for my life. I write it down in the front of my Bible to help me stay focused. One year in September, I had come to the point of earnestly praying for help in the area of true worship. It is my practice to rise about 5:00am and have my prayer time. I awoke with a sense that the Lord was saying to me to go up on the barn roof. This kind of stuff doesn't happen to me, being a conservative and esteeming myself to be a reasonable man. But after some time of negotiation I obeyed. In other words I knew it was too early for any of the neighbors to see me. It was an unusually balmy morning for September. The sun had not yet risen but the first light was beginning to show and I could distinguish the horizon. As I stood on the roof gazing into the eastern sky, the moon was just a sliver and directly below it was the morning star. The fragrance of autumn calmly blew in my face and a Psalm of David came to mind:

"When I consider thy heavens, the work of thy fingers,
the moon and the stars, which thou hast ordained;
What is man, that thou art mindful of him?
and the son of man, that thou visitest him"
  (Psa. 8:3–4)

I laid down on the roof in speechless adoration of my Creator God. I sensed a cleansing from the top of my head to the bottom of my feet. I was in no hurry to leave and even after I climbed down, I knew I had worshiped in spirit and in truth.

At the risk of sharing this experience, the profound truth I learned was; creation can provide opportunities to spontaneously worship the Creator in spirit and in truth. We are not supposed to worship the stars, but the Maker of the stars. We are not supposed to worship creation in any way, but instead the Creator. I can smell the fragrance of curing alfalfa in summer and instantly worship the One who gave that blessed aroma. I can hear the song of the first birds in spring , see a sunset, hear the wind in the trees, and many other often ignored spectaculars of creation and burst into glorious worship of the One who made and preserves them all. Few things prepare the soldier for battle better then true worship. I would love to spend more time here but before moving on I'll leave you this verse, "Thou, even thou, art Lord alone; thou hast made heaven, the heaven of heavens, with all their host, the earth, and all things that are in it, the seas, and all that is in them, and thou preserveth them all; and the host of heaven worshippeth thee" (Neh. 9:6).

A Will to Fight

If a soldier shows up for battle with nothing more than the shield of faith, the sword of the Spirit, and a will to fight, he will do serious damage to the enemy. If he shows up dressed in full armor with 21 weapons in hand yet with no will to fight he will be easily taken captive. Many times a superiorly talented athlete who is apathetic will sit on the bench and watch a far less talented athlete play with heart.

Resisting the devil can be exhausting work. Though we can be assured of victory every time we stand, we can't be assured we will stand every time. When we submit ourselves to God and resist the devil he will flee but what about the times we give place to the devil and he takes the day?

"Neither give place to the devil" (Eph. 4:27). In this portion of Scripture, Paul is clearly speaking to Christians about dealing with sin in their lives. He wouldn't have given this admonition of not to give place to the devil if it were impossible for us to do it. At times, Satan can take what may seem to be a small loss, use it to his advantage and drive us into a wilderness experience. Satan loves the wilderness, it is his favorite haunt. "For he had commanded the unclean spirit to come out of the man. For often it had caught him: and he was kept bound with chains and fetters; and he broke the bonds, and was driven of the demon into the wilderness" (Lu. 8:29). The wilderness is a horrible wasteland of unbelief, hopelessness, despair, oppression, loneliness, where one feels abandoned, confused, disoriented, aimless, and helpless with a dark depressing weight on their soul. Many a good soldier has lost his will to fight in the wilderness. While there they have become vulnerable to some of the most destructive assaults of the devil.

David the warrior knew what it was to find himself in a

dry and thirsty land with no water. But David also knew how to recover his will to fight and eventually return to the front lines. David had mastered the art of encouraging himself in the Lord his God. 1 Samuel 30 records a scene where the Amalekites had invaded Ziklag and made off with all of David's family, the families of all his men, as well as their possessions. The enemy had scored a big victory. Satan wasted no time in taking advantage of the situation and quickly turned the hearts of David's men against him. His comrades who at one time had fought alongside him were now talking about stoning him. "… but David encouraged himself in the Lord his God" (v. 6). An encouraged David went to prayer and asked God what to do. God gave him the answer and he followed it. He told his men they would have to postpone the stoning until after he had retrieved their families and his. The men rallied and joined him in pursuit of the enemy. Together they recovered all that had been taken.

There are times when others encourage us in the Lord and we recover our will to fight, but it is good to have a plan should you find yourself all alone. My plan may not be very profound but it has brought me out of the wilderness on many occasions. It is summed up in one word: Eternity! Life has its tribulations, but life lasts but a moment. Life is a handbreadth, a vapor, a shadow that passeth away. "Man that is born of a woman is of few days and full of trouble" (Job 14:1). Life is short and death is certain. "And as it is appointed unto men once to die, but after this the judgment" (Heb. 9:27). There is a life after this temporal one. It is an eternal one. In the end the gates of hell shall not prevail, so why should they now? Eternity, Eternity, Eternity, helps me recover my will to fight. Though Satan be allowed to do his worst, I know how things turn out and so does he. "And the devil that deceived them was cast into the lake of fire and brimstone, where the beast and the false prophet are, and shall be tormented day and night forever and ever" (Rev. 20:10).

THANKFULNESS

A number of years ago I heard a godly old man give a reply that stuck with me. He responded uniquely to the generic American greeting, "Hey, how are you doing?" I knew he had many of the afflictions that accompany older people yet he answered meekly and clearly, "Better than I deserve." Oh, how I have used that perspective to pound the devil when he would tempt me to be ungrateful. Anything short of hell is better than I deserve. With this perspective you can say that you are either up or getting up. It is hard to keep a thankful person down. The trial of our faith is but the flame that brings the dross to the surface to be removed by the goldsmith. "That the trial of your faith, being much more precious than of the gold that perisheth, though it be tried with fire, might be found unto praise and honor and glory at the appearing of Jesus Christ, whom having not seen, ye love; in whom, though ye see him not, yet believing, ye rejoice with joy unspeakable and full of glory" (1 Pet. 1:7–8).

A favorite saying of my dad is, "You don't appreciate feeling good 'til you're sick, and you don't appreciate your car 'til it don't run." That simple little statement is an honest reflection of human nature which Satan loves to take advantage of to turn us into complainers. Every person who consciously determines to be thankful will have the enemy on his heels before the battle really gets going.

The Apostle Paul gave us an insight from his own personal struggle. The specific issue isn't clear but his response is. "And lest I should be exalted above measure through the abundance of the revelations, there was given to me a thorn in the flesh, the messenger of Satan to buffet me, lest I should be exalted above measure. For this thing I besought the Lord thrice, that it might depart from me. And he said unto me, My grace is sufficient for thee: for my strength is made perfect in weakness. Most gladly therefore will I rather glory in my infirmities, that the power of Christ may rest upon me. Therefore I take pleasure in infirmities, in reproaches, in necessities, in persecutions, in distress for Christ's sake: for when I am weak, then I am strong" (2 Cor. 12:7–10). When thankfulness becomes our response to the enemy's assaults, it is as if he is shooting himself in the foot. There is no better way to put him to flight than to maintain a healthy use of thankfulness. "In everything give thanks: for this is the will of God in Christ Jesus concerning you" (1 Thes. 5:18). It doesn't say be thankful FOR everything, just be thankful IN everything. Whether I am in a fix because of the world, the flesh, or the devil, regardless of the arena, if God be for me then who cares who's against me? "Be anxious for nothing; but in everything by prayer and supplication with thanksgiving let your request be made known unto God. And the peace of God, which passeth all understanding, shall keep your hearts and minds through Christ Jesus" (Phil. 4:6–7). This weapon is most needed in the hard times. However, we aren't likely to be accurate with it unless its use is perfected in the good times. Oh, let us give thanks unto the Lord for He is good. To my shame I am not nearly as good with this weapon as I should be. I take far too much for granted. Even when I have prayed and the Lord has granted my request, there have been times I have forgotten to give thanks. Lord, I determine to be more mindful of Your goodness and consciously give thanks to You.

WONDER

The poor atheist has nothing above himself to excite awe or wonder. His entire reason for existence lies within himself alone. He has no fear, no trembling, and no reverence for anything eternal. His sad assumption of life is that we are nothing more than worm food, intellectual fertilizer for the next generation, and a mindless repetition of life that has no other purpose than the propagation of the species.

When Solomon in all his wisdom looked at life through the lens of human wisdom alone, he came to the same conclusion as the atheist. He was near the end of his life; he had drifted far from God when he wrote Ecclesiastes. The book is filled with the pessimistic words of a cynical old man who had lost the wonder of God. Solomon's theme is vanity of vanities, all is vanity and vexation of spirit. Here was a man with wealth and power, prestige, and complete success in the eyes of the world, yet he found life was empty and without meaning. There was no eternal value. For him there was nothing new under the sun which is quite contrary to the promises of God in Holy Scripture. "Therefore if any man be in Christ, he is a new creation; old things are passed away; behold, all things are become new" (2 Cor. 5:17). We can come into the very presence of God by a new and living way that was made possible through Christ (see Heb. 10:19–21). We can put off the old man and put on the new (see Col. 3:9–11). We can walk in the newness of life (see Rom. 6:4). His mercies are new every morning (see Lam. 3:22–23). And one day there will be a new heaven and a new earth (2 Pet. 3:13, Rev. 21:1–8).

I have learned to nurture wonder, mainly by pondering the love of God. It is a powerful weapon against the lies of the devil which are always to the contrary. "But God who is rich in mercy, for his great love with which he loved us, even when we were dead in sins, hath made us alive together with Christ (by grace ye are saved;)" (Eph. 2:4–5). "In this was manifested the love of God toward us, because that God sent his only begotten Son into the world, that we might live through him. Herein is love, not that we loved God, but that he loved us, and sent his Son to be the propitiation for our sins. Beloved, if God so loved us, we ought also to love one another" (1 John 4:9–11). I so enjoy pondering verses like John 3:16, Romans 5:8, 1 John 4:19, and 1 Corinthians 13. More often than not I end up singing that great old hymn

"I stand amazed in the presence
of Jesus the Nazarene,
and wonder how he could love me,
a sinner, condemned, unclean.

How marvelous! How wonderful!
And my song shall ever be:
How marvelous! How wonderful
is my Savior's love for me!"

"But ye are a chosen generation, a royal priesthood, an holy nation, a people of his own: that ye should show forth the praises of him who hath called you out of darkness into his marvelous light" (1 Pet. 2:9).

In my opinion the most unbelieved doctrine in the Bible is that of man's total depravity. Could it be we don't believe how dark the darkness in us really is because we have lost the wonder and marvel of God's love? Gypsy Smith, a well-known evangelist of the 19th century, tirelessly preached the gospel throughout the world. In his later years, he was asked how he kept the exhausting pace of ministry. His only response was, "I never lost the wonder of it all."

Many love songs have been written throughout time; it is even said people sing about what they love. I know next to nothing about music but when I am moved to wonder at God and stand in awe of Him, I do love to sing. A good way to close this weapon is with a great old hymn of Charles Wesley:

> *"And can it be that I should gain*
> *an interest in the Savior's blood?*
> *Died he for me, who cause his pain—*
> *For me, who Him to death pursued?*
> *Amazing love! How can it be,*
> *That thou, my God, shouldest die for me?*
> *Amazing love! How can it be,*
> *That thou, my God, shouldest die for me?"*

LOOKING FOR THE BLESSED HOPE

When the Christian soldier lives with a healthy expectancy of Christ's return, it is as if he is saying to Satan, "Take your best shot now, for the day is coming when you are going to pay for every assault you have ever made." The return of Christ is as fundamental to the Christian faith as the resurrection. If you don't believe one then you don't believe the other. The return of Christ is an obvious part of the Apostles' doctrine. The Church is built upon the foundation of the Apostles and the Prophets. There have always been mockers from the day of Pentecost until now. According to Scripture there will be mockers right up until the day He comes. "Knowing this first, that there shall come in the last days scoffers, walking after their own lusts, and saying, Where is the promise of his coming? for since the fathers fell asleep, all things continue as they were from the beginning of creation" (2 Pet. 3:3–4).

As Paul preached the gospel to the intellectuals of Athens, the majority listened to him right up until he spoke of the day of Christ's return. "Because he hath appointed a day, in which he will judge the world in righteousness by that man whom he hath ordained; concerning which he hath given assurance unto all men, in that he hath raised him from the dead. And when they heard of the resurrection of the dead, some mocked: and others said, We will hear thee again of this matter. So Paul departed from among them. Nevertheless certain men joined him, and believed, among whom were Dionysius the Areopagite, and a woman named Damaris, and others with them" (Acts 17:31–34).

Paul told Titus to teach people to deny ungodliness and worldly lusts and live soberly in this old world. On the heels of that admonition he gave this incentive to strengthen them. "Looking for that blessed hope, and the glorious appearing of the great God and our Savior Jesus Christ" (v. 2:13). Likewise, the great weight of Paul's final words to Timothy were based upon the imminent return of Christ. "I charge thee therefore before God, and the Lord Jesus Christ, who shall judge the living and the dead at his appearing and his kingdom" (2 Tim. 4:1). The Apostle John affirmed the return of Christ in his letter. "Beloved, now are we the children of God, and it doth not yet appear what we shall be: but we know that, when he shall appear, we shall be like him; for we shall see him as he is. And every man that hath this hope in him purifieth himself, even as he is pure" (1 John 3:2–3).

As the disciples witnessed the ascension of Christ into heaven, two men in white apparel, most likely angels, said to them, "Ye men of Galilee: why stand ye gazing up into heaven? this same Jesus, who is taken up from you into heaven, shall so come in like manner as ye have seen him go into heaven" (Acts 1:11). The writer of Hebrews exhorts the Christian to get all the more serious about the battle as he sees this day approaching. "For yet a little while, and he that shall come will come, and will not tarry" (v. 10:37). There isn't one thing Satan and his entire host can do to stop it. When the spiritual battle is raging, don't hesitate to use it against him. It will strengthen your position and weaken his.

CHAPTER SEVEN

TEARING DOWN STRONGHOLDS

Any area of moral weakness in one's life where Satan has taken advantage of the opportunity to tighten his grip will become a stronghold, an area of sin where he has had time to dig in and fortify himself. Satan may have been given the opportunity through generational sins or some door we have ignorantly or willfully left open to his influence. These can and must be torn down.

When a person is born again he has a brand new status before God. He is accepted in the Beloved and complete in Christ. "To the praise of the glory of his grace, through which he hath made us accepted in the Beloved" (Eph. 1:6). "And ye are complete in him, who is the head of all principality and power" (Col. 2:10). The penalty of the Christian's sin is paid in full and the power of sin has been broken, but the presence of sin is exactly the same. He wakes up in the same body, in the same sinful world, only now he has made an enemy out of one who used to be his ally. Yes, he is sealed with the Holy Spirit of promise and the eternal destiny of his soul is secure unto the day of redemption. "That we should be to the praise of his glory, who first trusted in Christ. In whom ye also trusted, after ye heard the word of truth, the gospel of your salvation: in whom also after that ye believed, ye were sealed with that Holy Spirit of promise" (Eph. 1:12–13). "And grieve not the Holy Spirit of God, by whom ye are sealed unto the day of redemption" (Eph. 4:30). When he enters heaven, he will be beyond the devil's reach, but while he is on earth the war for the testimony of his soul is on.

When I committed my life to Christ, I had a filthy mouth. That stronghold fell, like Jericho, in a single week. The enemy was routed. That is not the case with every believer. Some Christians never experience a Jericho. For many believers the stronghold of swearing comes down slowly, one brick at a time. I know of believers who were set free from alcohol or drug addiction the day they came to Christ. I know of many others where it took months or years of hard fighting for the stronghold to come down. Every person who comes to Christ would like a quick victory over their strongholds, but if that occurred who would learn how to wage a good warfare? Who would experience using his weapons in the fight of faith?

A Spiritual Stronghold

"For though we walk in the flesh, we do not war after the flesh: (For the weapons of our warfare are not carnal, but mighty through God to the pulling down of strongholds)" (2 Cor. 10:3–4). Notice how the Apostle Paul includes himself as a warring soldier by using the plural pronouns "we" and "our." He is writing to the believers at Corinth of whom he said in his first letter, "I thank my God always on your behalf, for the grace of God which is given you by Jesus Christ; that in everything ye are enriched by him, in all utterance, and in all knowledge; even as the testimony of Christ was confirmed in you: So that ye come behind in no gift; waiting for the coming of our Lord Jesus Christ: who shall also confirm you unto the end, that ye may be blameless in the day of our Lord Jesus Christ. God is faithful, by who ye were called unto the fellowship of his Son Jesus Christ our Lord" (1 Cor. 1:4–9). It would seem from this text that Paul is saying a Christian can have an area of their life controlled by an evil spirit. A spiritual stronghold that needs to be attacked, dismantled and conquered. One where the Christian soldier needs to wear spiritual armor, use spiritual weapons with spiritual strategies, and spiritual perseverance. Theology often lacks clarity without examples. The following will be a short list of examples of some of the strongholds Christians face. I trust this glimpse will lend further meaning to 2 Corinthians 10:3–4.

The Stronghold of Fear

I know of people who, before coming to Christ, had become heavily involved in horror movies. They had become fascinated and even addicted to the rush that fear gave them. As they began their new life in the Lord they turned away from the movies, but a new unwanted terror seem to grip them. They confessed fear of the darkness and fear of being alone. Many other fears related to the things they had seen in their past plagued them. This was not a flesh and blood battle and they knew it. As they gained knowledge of spiritual warfare, the weapons came out and the fight was on. "For God hath not given us the spirit of fear; but of power, and of love, and of a sound mind" (2 Tim.1:7). Though I have not struggled with that kind of fear, I have had my own fears to deal with: fear of people, fear of failure, fear of rejection, and fear of the unknown. Without Christ and His power for the battle I would never have conquered the stronghold of fear. There is no way I would have a public preaching ministry and constantly be with people, many of whom I don't know, without the weapons God provides. In spiritual warfare, God delights in moving us out of who we are and growing us into someone we never could have dreamed of being.

The Stronghold of Greed

Most of us are tempted to get our identity from what we do or what we own rather than from who we are. This opens a big door for Satan to drive us into the wilderness of greed. Greed evidences itself in many ways but none more obviously than in the pursuit of riches. The love of money is the root of all types of evil. It has pushed many people into all kinds of destructive lifestyles far from God's design for their lives. Many marriages and homes have been sacrificed on the altar of money and the deceitfulness of riches. It may start out as only a foothold but it can quickly develop into a stronghold. From there Satan will use it to rob the believer of the manifold riches of Christ. For instance, the believer could be tempted to begin to compromise his standards of honesty and even stoop to embezzling funds. Though he is never caught, Satan has him in chains and there is barrenness in his soul.

Just because a person is wealthy doesn't mean he has a stronghold of greed. A believer may be poverty stricken and still find Satan thriving in a stronghold of greed in his life. The spiritual battle is on and warfare is declared. "Let him that stole steal no more, but rather let him labor, working with his hands the thing which is good, that he may have to give to him that needeth" (Eph. 4:28). When a person becomes a hoarder, it's a sure sign of a spiritual stronghold. It may come to prying Satan's grip off a finger at a time. Learning to see another's needs and desiring to meet those needs is a powerful weapon in that battle.

Coming to the understanding of stewardship is another powerful weapon. I remember coming to the place where I realized that everything I owned and had worked for was really God's. It was the Lord Who had given me the strength and ability to work, so all I had acquired really was a gift from Him. It was powerfully freeing to become an overseer of the affairs and possession of God. It's all His, even my wife and family. I am God's steward. At times the devil still tries to get me to think otherwise, but he no longer has control over that place in my life. There is a whole new world of liberty when the stronghold of greed comes down.

THE STRONGHOLD OF BITTERNESS

Bitterness is a poison we drink hoping it will kill somebody else. "Looking diligently lest any man fail of the grace of God; lest any root of bitterness springing up trouble you, and by it many be defiled" (Heb. 12:15). Bitterness is the result of holding a grudge or being unwilling to forgive. Forgiveness is an act of obedience to the command and example of Christ. "And be ye kind one to another, tenderhearted, forgiving one another, even as God for Christ's sake hath forgiven you" (Eph. 4:32). Satan will use unforgiveness to build a fortress against your soul. Nothing but a spiritual wasteland awaits the person who will not forgive. Every time they justify themselves for not forgiving their offender the devil will say, "Amen." The enemy will give more and more reasons to hold onto the grudge. Bitterness will dry your bones and destroy your health, physically, mentally, and emotionally. This stronghold has got to come down.

Spiritual warfare is on, let the battle begin! A number of

years ago I was struggling with bitterness against another pastor. My walk with the Lord had slowed to a crawl and I knew I had to forgive him. I went through the clinical motions which are a step in the right direction but my heart was slow to catch up. I memorized Matthew 18 and began to meditate on it. It is a big gun in this battle. If I had owed God a hundred million dollars and He forgave me every dime of the debt, how could I not forgive someone who, in comparison, owed me a measly one hundred dollars? Another brick in the stronghold had come down.

Around the same time, I met a man horribly tormented by the devil with unforgiveness. He had caught his wife in adultery. He was so distraught he even had thoughts of killing her. I talked and prayed with him for about an hour. I led him through a prayer of forgiveness. There was no denying this was spiritual warfare on the front line. Forgiveness was not easy, but when he saw it as his only hope, the process of tearing down the stronghold began. Eventually he came to freedom and his marriage was restored. I was learning the only thing harder than forgiveness is unforgiveness.

Finally, I went to my pastor friend and told him my sin. I asked him to forgive me, which he did. In the process of time I learned a valuable lesson that has served me well ever since. Satan lost his stronghold and I am a better soldier for having fought that battle.

THE STRONGHOLD OF UNBELIEF

Believing is the only cure for unbelief. That statement may not sound very profound, but nonetheless, it is true. We are born unbelievers; we are born again by believing the claims of Jesus as the Christ. "For God sent not is Son into the world to condemn the world; but that the world through him might be saved. He that believeth on him is not condemned: but he that believeth not is condemned already, because he hath not believed in the name of the only begotten Son of God" (John 3:17–18).

Over the years I have become amazed at how strongly people believe in what they don't believe. Several years ago I was preaching at a Bible conference. I was not the only speaker but I was responsible for three of the messages that weekend. After my first message, I was talking with people and a man made the statement, "I don't believe in God!" I knew he wanted me to enter into an intellectual debate over the existence of God. I chose rather to look into his eyes and wait for him to speak further. He hadn't asked me a question, so I didn't feel bound to respond. In a short time he dropped his eye contact with me and I resumed speaking with someone else. After my second message, I saw him in line and wondered what he might say. He eventually had the opportunity and made the statement, "I don't believe the Bible!" I knew he wanted me to try and prove to him the authority of Scripture, and I also knew no amount of proof would convince him. I looked at him without speaking. He hadn't asked me a question so I didn't see any wisdom in entering the debate. Eventually he dropped his eye contact and I resumed a conversation with someone else. After my third message, I saw him again. I was learning what he didn't believe and realized he had strong faith in what he didn't believe. In his third and final statement to me he said, "I don't believe in hell!" As kindly as I could, I said, "After you die you will believe in all three. I pray that you do not wait that long for if you do it will be too late. There are no unbelievers on the other side of the grave." I am sad to say he walked away continuing to believe what he didn't believe. "And some believed the things which were spoken, and some believed not" (Acts 28:24).

When given the opportunity Satan will build a sturdy stronghold of unbelief. A powerful way to begin to tear that stronghold down is by following the Scriptural example of a common man. His son was tormented by the devil and no one had been able to help him. He had heard about Jesus and His power over the devil. He brought his son and asked for help. "Jesus said unto him, If thou canst believe, all things are possible to him that believeth. And straightway the father of the child cried out, and said with tears, Lord, I believe; help thou mine unbelief" (Mk. 9:23–24). Jesus set his son free. That same power is still available to all who will only believe.

In Conclusion

The book of Joshua records only one Jericho as they entered the land; the remainder of his book is a record of military strategies where the land was conquered with the edge of the sword and plenty of hard fighting. Moses encouraged Joshua to be strong and trust in the Lord, for He would surely give them the land though there were many fortified cities to defeat. They conquered the majority of the land but not every walled city came down; some strongholds remained in the land of Israel. Joshua failed to conquer the city of the Jebusites. It wasn't until the generation of David that it was conquered. David renamed the city Jerusalem, which became called by God's Name, the city of the great King and the city of Zion. Jerusalem is the greatest city on earth and is still being fought over today. Every war ever fought has behind it a spiritual dynamic, regardless of the scale. We are called as Christians to a spiritual battle against Satan and his host. The Apostle Paul tells us to be strong in the Lord and the power of His might, put on the full armor of God, and enter the fray with our faces to the enemy. We have been delivered from the dominion of darkness and translated into the kingdom of His dear Son. "For ye were once darkness, but now are ye light in the Lord; walk as children of light" (Eph. 5:8). Take courage in the fact that it's a blessing just being in the fight. Though the battle may be hard, the victory is ours. "But thanks be to God, who giveth us the victory through our Lord Jesus Christ. Therefore, my beloved brethren, be ye steadfast, unmovable, always abounding in the work of the Lord, forasmuch as ye know that your labor is not in vain in the Lord" (1 Cor. 15:57–58).

God bless you as you press on in your journey of faith.

CPSIA information can be obtained at www.ICGtesting.com
Printed in the USA
BVOW081647030812

296990BV00004B/2/P